Comfort Zone

Escape Your Comfort Zone and
Thrive as an Introvert

*(Make an Escape Plan, Map Your Journey and
Build a Life That Lights You Up)*

Gary McDaniel

Published By **Jenna Olsen**

Gary McDaniel

All Rights Reserved

Comfort Zone: Escape Your Comfort Zone and Thrive as an Introvert (Make an Escape Plan, Map Your Journey and Build a Life That Lights You Up)

ISBN 978-1-7772636-7-6

No part of this guidebook shall be reproduced in any form without permission in writing from the publisher except in the case of brief quotations embodied in critical articles or reviews.

Legal & Disclaimer

The information contained in this book is not designed to replace or take the place of any form of medicine or professional medical advice. The information in this book has been provided for educational & entertainment purposes only.

The information contained in this book has been compiled from sources deemed reliable, and it is accurate to the best of the Author's knowledge; however, the Author cannot guarantee its accuracy and validity and cannot be held liable for any errors or omissions. Changes are periodically made to this book. You must consult your doctor or get professional medical advice before using any of the suggested remedies, techniques, or information in this book.

Upon using the information contained in this book, you agree to hold harmless the Author from and against any damages, costs, and expenses, including any legal fees potentially resulting from the application of any of the information provided by this guide. This disclaimer applies to any damages or injury caused by the use and application, whether directly or indirectly, of any advice or information presented, whether for breach of contract, tort, negligence, personal injury, criminal intent, or under any other cause of action.

You agree to accept all risks of using the information presented inside this book. You need to consult a professional medical practitioner in order to ensure you are both able and healthy enough to participate in this program.

Table Of Contents

Chapter 1: The Comfort Zone 1

Chapter 2: Confronting Fear and Embracing Discomfort 23

Chapter 3: The Power Of Perspective 50

Chapter 4: Navigating Transitions 72

Chapter 5: Strategies for Overcoming Obstacles 98

Chapter 6: Why Comfort Isn't Always Best 110

Chapter 7: Developing a Growth Mindset 123

Chapter 8: Navigating Setbacks and Challenges 137

Chapter 9: Creating a Vision for Your Future 148

Chapter 10: The Value of Rest and Rejuvenation 160

Chapter 11: The Power of Embracing Discomfort 171

Chapter 1: The Comfort Zone

Understanding its Limitations and Pitfalls

Welcome to the wacky international of the consolation vicinity, in which comfortable sports and acquainted conduct create a bubble of contentment. While it may feel like the final stable haven, we have to no longer overlook the restrictions and pitfalls that lurk internal its comfortable embody. In this whimsical exploration, we are able to embark on a joyous adventure to understand the hidden dangers of the consolation place, all even as preserving our spirits excessive and our smiles sizable.

The "Cozy but Stagnant" Quicksand Picture the comfort quarter as a marshmallow-crammed pit of quicksand At first, sinking into its marsh mallow depths may enjoy comfortable and stable, however as time is going by way of the usage of, we recognize that consolation can breed complacency.

We become stagnant, stuck in the marshmallow dust, now not capable of transport beforehand. It's like looking to run a marathon at the same time as carrying fluffy slippers!

The "Fear of the Unknown" Roller Coaster Within the comfort place, fear of the unknown is a wild curler coaster revel in. We strap ourselves in, hesitating to take that exhilarating plunge into uncertainty. But because the roller coaster climbs better and higher, we pass over out on thrilling twists, turns, and breathtaking perspectives. The worry of the unknown will become a barrier, holding us decrease returned from experiencing the magic that lies simply beyond.

The "Monotonous Hamster Wheel" Circus In the consolation place, lifestyles can revel in like an limitless circus act, with normal obligations and predictable patterns spinning us spherical and round. We come to be hamsters on wheels, tirelessly walking but going nowhere. It's like acting the equal acrobatic hints on a each day basis without ambitious to step onto the tightrope of recent disturbing conditions and thrilling adventures.

The "Bubble of False Security" Illusion The consolation zone creates a bubble of faux safety, shielding us from the realities of lifestyles. We can also feel blanketed within its confines, but it's miles like residing in a fantastical bubble that separates us from the actual reviews and boom waiting genuinely out of doors. Bursting that bubble may be frightening, but it's the nice way to genuinely interact with the arena and find out our complete functionality.

The "Dreams on Hold" Ferris Wheel Within the consolation place, dreams often sit down down on a desk sure Ferris wheel, going spherical and round however never commencing. We watch from under, longing to hop on and revel in the breathtaking heights of success and achievement. It's time to accumulate the braveness to step out of doors our consolation zones, board that Ferris wheel, and permit it spin us to new horizons of fulfillment and happiness.

The "Regret Factory" Funhouse If we continue to be in the comfort location, we risk getting into the regret production unit, a funhouse of overlooked opportunities and unfulfilled desires. We wander through hallways filled with mirrors reflecting what might have been, surrounded through the echoing whispers of "What if?" It's time to break loose from this funhouse, to encompass the unknown and create a existence wherein regrets are changed with radiant smiles.

The "Magic Lies Beyond" Wonderland Beyond the comfort sector lies a wonderland of boom, discovery, and infinite possibilities. It's like moving into a fantastical realm in which colourful colorings paint the sky, and adventures beckon from every nook. It's a place in which we are able to examine, attain, and create, all at the same time as embracing the exhilarating unpredictability of lifestyles. So, permit's depart the comfort place behind and enter this wondrous international with massive-eyed surprise and a mischievous grin.

As we bid farewell to the comfortable comforts of our comfort zones, let us not neglect that there's a playful international ready beyond. By information the policies and pitfalls of the consolation area, we are able to free up ourselves from complacency and embark on a thrilling journey of increase and self-discovery. So, my adventurous pal, let's harm free from the marshmallow dust, triumph over the concern-crammed curler coaster, and burst the bubble of faux protection. Together, we can discover the wonderland that lies actually beyond, giggling, studying, and residing existence to the fullest inside the most delightfully a laugh manner feasible.

Defining the Comfort Zone: What Keeps Us Stuck?

Welcome to the whimsical realm of the comfort area, an area wherein comfortable slippers, fluffy blankets, and acquainted workouts create a haven of contentment. But what if I instructed you that inner this realm lies a hidden treasure trove of untapped capability and exhilarating possibilities? In this first-rate exploration, we will embark on a joyous adventure to outline the consolation place in a a laugh and motivational manner, in which we discover that consolation and increase can coexist in the maximum high-quality of strategies.

The Cozy Wonderland of Comfort Imagine the consolation place as a paranormal wonderland, packed with fluffy clouds, warmness cocoa, and snuggly blankets. It's an area wherein we revel in comfortable, surrounded thru familiar factors of hobby and sounds. Like slipping into your favored pajamas after a protracted day, the consolation place wraps us in a warmth consist of, supplying solace and rest.

Embracing the Power of Comfort Within the comfort sector, we find out secure haven from the hustle and bustle of normal lifestyles. It's a place wherein we are able to recharge, find out peace, and replenish our energy. Like a cup of tea on a moist day, the consolation sector nourishes our souls, permitting us to collect power and prepare for the adventures that lie in advance.

The Comfort Zone's Limitations While the comfort vicinity is a lovely retreat, it additionally has its barriers. If we stay interior its snug confines for too prolonged, we chance becoming stagnant and lacking out on the huge global outside. It's like snuggling in a mild cocoon, steady however isolated from the wonders and demanding situations that appearance earlier to us. It's time to break unfastened and encompass the adventure past!

Embracing the Discomfort of Growth Stepping beyond the consolation area may be each thrilling and nerve-wracking. It's like embarking on a exciting roller coaster journey, with twists, turns, and unexpected surprises. Yes, there can be pain, but it's miles interior that ache that actual growth and transformation rise up. It's like stretching your wings and chickening out, coming across new heights and competencies you in no manner knew existed.

Expanding the Boundaries of the Comfort Zone Instead of viewing the consolation region as a difficult and fast location, lets say it as an growing bubble. By little by little pushing the limits of our comfort vicinity, we open ourselves as lots as new critiques, abilties, and views. It's like which include colorful balloons to our bubble, filling it with the exhilaration and possibilities of the unknown.

The Thrill of Stepping Outside Stepping outdoor the consolation area is like stepping onto a colourful carnival halfway. The points of hobby, sounds, and smells fill us with anticipation and delight. It's an area in which we are able to venture ourselves, try new matters, and include the fun of the unknown. It's time to capture that cotton candy of courage and take a leap into the adventure that awaits!

Celebrating Each Step of Growth As we challenge beyond the comfort sector, it is critical to rejoice every step we take. Each second of courage, each enjoy that pushes our obstacles, merits popularity and applause. It's like triumphing a crammed animal at a carnival endeavor—the pride and delight in our accomplishments gasoline our desire to keep exploring and increasing our comfort sector.

Dear adventurer, inside the consolation region lies a global of coziness and contentment, but it's far outdoor its limitations that our right capability and boom look ahead to. Let's encompass the energy of consolation whilst retaining our eyes open to the wonders that lie past. With a playful spirit and a sprinkle of motivation, we are able to navigate the roller coaster of growth, developing our comfort location and embracing the joyous adventure of existence. So, allow's embark in this first-rate journey together, understanding that inside the balance of consolation and exploration, we're able to create a existence filled with each coziness and infinite opportunities.

The consolation region, with its comfortable familiarity and experience of safety, can be a charming place to linger. However, it often turns into a entice that keeps us stuck, stopping non-public boom and stifling our ability. Let's delve into some reasons why we discover it tough to break free from the comfort area, with relatable examples that illustrate those tendencies.

One of the number one factors that hold us rooted in the comfort region is the concern of failure. We worry that stepping outdoor our acquainted boundaries may also furthermore result in mistakes, setbacks, or embarrassment. This fear can take place in severa regions of lifestyles, which consist of pursuing new career opportunities, starting a commercial enterprise, or maybe pursuing non-public relationships. For example, someone may additionally furthermore hesitate to apply for their dream project because they fear rejection or worry about now not meeting expectancies. This worry of failure will become a powerful pressure that maintains them definitely caught in their present day sports, in location of taking a soar of faith.

A loss of self belief also can contribute to our reluctance to depart the comfort zone. We may also moreover doubt our skills, query whether or now not we're "accurate sufficient," or fear that we are going to be not capable of deal with the demanding situations that consist of venturing into the unknown. As a cease result, we take delivery of what feels stable and acquainted, preserving off conditions that require us to step outside our consolation area. For instance, a person with a passion for writing may also additionally moreover hesitate to percentage their artwork with others due to a lack of self perception in their capabilities, opting to hold their information hidden in area of taking the chance of rejection or grievance.

Human beings are creatures of addiction, and we virtually gravitate within the route of what feels snug. The comfort area offers a feel of stability and predictability, which can be tough to allow go of. We come to be attached to sporting activities, behavior, and environments that we're acquainted with, even though they now not serve our growth or deliver us proper success. For instance, a person can also remain in a technique they dislike as it gives a everyday profits and a enjoy of safety, even though it stifles their ardour and functionality for non-public increase.

Change can be unsettling, despite the fact that it has the functionality to purpose fantastic results. The consolation area acts as a defend in competition to the uncertainties and annoying conditions that include alternate. We resist leaving this sector because it calls for us to conform, examine new abilties, and face atypical conditions. For instance, a person might also additionally moreover resist transferring to a today's metropolis or u . S . A ., even though it gives exciting opportunities, because of the reality they worry the discomfort of converting to a one of a kind surroundings and constructing new social connections.

External impacts, together with peer pressure and societal expectancies, can also make contributions to our reluctance to step outdoor the comfort region. We may additionally revel in pressured to conform to societal norms or meet the expectations of others, despite the truth that doing so hinders our non-public growth. For instance, a person also can withstand pursuing a modern career path due to the fact their circle of relatives or friends anticipate them to pursue a extra traditional, financially strong career.

Although the comfort place affords a experience of protection and familiarity, it could prevent us from attaining our complete capability and experiencing private growth. Fear of failure, lack of self warranty, attachment to comfort, resistance to trade, and external pressures are some of the factors that hold us stuck inner this quarter. However, recognizing and knowledge those affects lets in us to challenge them, step out of doors our comfort location, and embark on a adventure of self-discovery, success, and private development. It is within the ones moments of ache and uncertainty that we regularly locate the remarkable opportunities for boom and transformation.

The Illusion of Security: The Price of Staying Within Comfort Zones

Welcome, my adventurous buddy, to a exquisite exploration of the consolation zone and the phantasm of safety it offers. While the consolation location also can look like a solid haven, we're about to locate the hidden rate we pay for staying inside its confines. In this first-rate adventure, we are capable of dance with metaphors and embody playful examples to shed slight at the risks of clinging to the consolation location. So, clutch your cape of braveness and allow's unmask the phantasm of protection collectively!

The Fortress of Familiarity Picture the comfort place as a citadel, with strong walls and a moat of familiar workouts. It can also enjoy like an impenetrable castle, providing a enjoy of safety and stability. But what lies past those walls? Adventure, increase, and exciting possibilities look beforehand to folks who dare to challenge out. It's time to don our capes and soar past the fortress partitions.

The Spiderweb of Stagnation Within the consolation place, time can experience like a sticky spiderweb, trapping us in a country of stagnation. We can also moreover discover ourselves stuck within the identical routine, day in and day experience, like a spider awaiting its subsequent meal. We're cushty, however we are additionally lacking out on the colorful tapestry of stories that lie really beyond the net. It's time to break loose from the sticky strands and embody the colourful international outside.

The Magic Shop of Missed Opportunities Imagine the comfort place as a amazing magic maintain, complete of shelves of not noted opportunities. We wander thru the aisles, watching at the unrealized dreams and untaken chances. We may be tempted with the useful resource of the flashy distractions of safety and familiarity, but inside the again of those illusions lies a trove of unexplored wonders. It's time to location on our magician's hat and conjure up the courage to seize those opportunities earlier than they vanish.

The Carousel of Regret Within the comfort sector, there may be a carousel that maintains us spinning in circles of regret. We hop onto the colorful horses, going round and spherical, but never moving ahead. Each time we pass through an opportunity to grow, a whisper of regret tugs at our hearts. It's time to step off the carousel, embody the uncertainty, and embark on a exciting adventure in which regrets are modified with joyous recollections.

The Puzzle of Potential The consolation location is kind of a puzzle with missing quantities. We also can have some quantities in location, supplying a feel of balance and familiarity, but the puzzle remains incomplete. The missing quantities represent untapped functionality, watching for us to assignment outdoor the consolation area and discover new dimensions of ourselves. It's time to build up those missing pieces and create a masterpiece that displays our actual abilties.

The Painted Path of Passion Within the consolation vicinity, the route in advance than us is painted with muted colours. It's predictable and stable, however lacks the vibrant hues of passion and pleasure. By stepping outdoor our comfort zones, we liberate a palette of possibilities. We can paint our very personal path with bold strokes of passion, developing a masterpiece that presentations our specific dreams and aspirations. It's time to dip our brushes into the paint of courage and permit our right colors shine.

The Carnival of Growth As we bid farewell to the phantasm of protection, we input a carnival of boom. It's a energetic, bustling location full of exhilarating rides, interesting video video games, and exciting disturbing situations. Each attraction beckons us to step outside our comfort zones and encompass the unknown. It's time to indulge within the carnival of increase, to experience the fun of latest critiques, and to have a laugh the boom of our comfort zones.

Dear adventurer, the comfort vicinity can also provide an phantasm of protection, however its charge is a lifestyles unfulfilled. By venturing past its confines, we release ourselves from the citadel of familiarity, ruin unfastened from the spiderweb of stagnation, and embody the magic keep of unnoticed possibilities. We step off the carousel of remorse and entire the puzzle of our ability. We paint our personal route with ardour and immerse ourselves in the carnival of growth. So, allow's put off the illusion of protection, dance with uncertainty, and embark on a adventure in which joy, success, and infinite opportunities assume.

Recognizing Signs of Stagnation and the Need for Change

In the symphony of existence, we frequently discover ourselves drifting along a familiar melody, snug in the sporting events and patterns that outline our existence. However, there comes a time whilst the tune starts offevolved offevolved to lose its vibrancy, and we experience the stirring of restlessness deep inner our souls. These are the signs and symptoms of stagnation, slight whispers urging us to recognize the need for change. In this adventure of self-discovery and motivation, we are capable of discover the diverse signs and symptoms of stagnation and learn how to embody the transformative strength of exchange. So, allow us to embark on this empowering quest and ignite the flame of motivation inside us.

The Soft Whisper of Discontent When we find out ourselves stuck in the rhythm of every day lifestyles, there is usually a smooth whisper of discontent that starts to resonate internal us. It is a quiet voice, gently nudging us to are attempting to find for added, to try for boom and progress. This discontent arises from a deep-seated preference for some component beyond the everyday, a yearning to interrupt free from the confines of our comfort location. It is an indication that change is beckoning us, urging us to embark on a current course of self-discovery and private improvement.

The Fading Spark of Passion Passion, like a high-quality flame, fuels our endeavors and fills our hearts with cause. However, whilst that flame begins offevolved to flicker and fade, it's far a clean indication that stagnation has set in. We can also moreover find out ourselves going through the motions, lacking the passion and zest that after fueled our interests. Recognizing this fading spark of ardour is a powerful catalyst for exchange. It prompts us to rekindle our hobbies, are looking for new stressful situations, and reignite the fireplace within us.

The Monotony of Routine Life's exercises may be every comforting and stifling. While they provide a experience of stability and predictability, they also can purpose a experience of monotony and complacency. When every day looks like a repeat of the final, without satisfaction and increase, it's far a easy signal that we need to interrupt unfastened from the shackles of regular. Embracing change technique embracing the unknown, stepping outside our comfort area, and searching out new critiques that invigorate our spirits.

Chapter 2: Confronting Fear And Embracing Discomfort

Life is a astounding tapestry woven with possibilities for boom and transformation. Yet, regularly we discover ourselves trapped in the confines of our consolation quarter, protected against the exhilaration and success that lie beyond its boundaries. In this motivational exploration, we are capable of delve into the transformative power of stepping out, confronting fear, and embracing ache. Like a compass guiding us in the direction of our real ability, we are able to find out the braveness, motivation, and resilience needed to embark on a adventure of personal growth. So, allow us to mission forth and free up the doors that bring about a life of brilliant possibilities.

The Clutches of Comfort: Comfort is a heat blanket that wraps us in familiarity and protection. However, whilst consolation turns into a jail, it stifles our boom and restricts our ability. Stepping out of our comfort sector is the critical issue to unlocking the chains that bind us. It calls for embracing uncertainty, embracing change, and embracing pain as catalysts for non-public development.

Confronting Fear: Fear is an high-quality adversary that frequently stands in our manner, paralyzing us and stopping us from taking the vital steps towards growth. However, it's miles critical to understand that fear is not an obstacle, however as an opportunity an invite to summon our inner power and face our disturbing conditions head-on. Confronting fear is a courageous act that propels us beforehand, permitting us to interrupt loose from the shackles that keep us once more.

The Power of Discomfort: Discomfort is the birthplace of increase and transformation. It is in the realm of pain that we discover the finest possibilities for self-discovery and personal development. By embracing ache, we amplify our horizons, push our limits, and uncover strengths we in no way knew existed. Stepping out into the unknown calls for a willingness to bear transient pain in exchange for lengthy-time period growth and success.

Embracing the Unknown: The unknown may be each thrilling and terrifying. It is a massive panorama of untapped capacity and limitless possibilities. Stepping into the unknown requires a mind-set shift, a willingness to include uncertainty and agree with in our potential to navigate uncharted waters. Embracing the unknown lets in us to faucet into our resilience, adaptability, and creativity, empowering us to conquer limitations and capture possibilities for non-public boom.

Embracing Failure as a Stepping Stone: Failure isn't the forestall, but a stepping stone on the path to achievement. It is through failure that we take a look at valuable lessons, gain resilience, and refine our techniques. Embracing failure way reframing our belief, statistics that every setback is an opportunity for boom and improvement. It requires resilience, perseverance, and an unwavering notion in our capability to upward thrust above adversity.

Cultivating a Growth Mindset: A boom mindset is the foundation for embracing soreness and confronting worry. It is the notion that our abilities and intelligence may be advanced through willpower, try, and a willingness to observe. Cultivating a increase mind-set way embracing stressful conditions, attempting to find remarks, and persisting inside the face of setbacks. It is a thoughts-set that fosters non-public growth, resilience, and a lifelong love for reading.

Celebrating the Journey Stepping out, confronting worry, and embracing pain is a non-stop journey, now not a holiday spot. It is critical to rejoice the small victories alongside the manner, acknowledging the development we make and the training we analyze. Celebrating the adventure reinforces our motivation, boosts our self-self assurance, and offers the fuel had to preserve pushing past our limits.

Dear adventurer, stepping out of our comfort area, confronting worry, and embracing ache is a transformative adventure that unlocks the doors to private growth, resilience, and success. It calls for courage, willpower, and a perception in our very very personal talents. As we embark in this adventure, allow us to bear in mind that the rewards some distance outweigh the temporary discomfort we also can stumble upon. By confronting our fears head-on, embracing the unknown, and cultivating a growth mindset, we set ourselves on a route of countless opportunities and first rate achievements. So, permit us to take that soar of faith, step into the sector of pain, and free up our right capacity.

Understanding Fear: Its Role and Influence in Our Lives

Fear is an interesting pressure that publications through our veins, igniting our senses and triggering a cascade of feelings. It may be every a paralyzing presence and a catalyst for boom. In this thrilling exploration, we're able to delve into the depths of fear, unraveling its complicated role and discovering how it is able to effect our lives. From the gripping memories of historic warriors to the cutting-edge-day-day triumphs of regular heroes, we will uncover the energy that fear holds and the manner it can be harnessed to unfastened up our proper capacity. So, fasten your seatbelts and put together to embark on a coronary coronary heart-pounding journey into the area of fear.

The Dance of Survival Fear is an ancient dance that has been choreographed internal us because of the truth the dawn of time. It is an instinctual response designed to shield us from threat and make certain our survival. Picture a fearless caveman, poised getting ready to a treacherous cliff, the adrenaline coursing via his veins as he contemplates the jump. Fear publications his moves, urging caution and permitting him to make break up-2d alternatives. It is a primal strain that drives us to are trying to find for safety and keep away from harm.

The Illusion of Fear While fear serves a important reason in our lives, it may moreover create illusions that restrict our development. It whispers recollections of worst-case eventualities, conjuring photographs of failure and humiliation. Imagine a budding entrepreneur, his coronary coronary coronary heart pounding with satisfaction and trepidation as he contemplates beginning his personal commercial agency. Fear wraps its tendrils spherical his desires, whispering doubts and uncertainties. Yet, he learns to distinguish among rational fears and irrational illusions, channeling the power of worry towards calculated risks and calculated success.

Fear as a Compass, Fear isn't first-rate a dilemma; it may be a compass that factors us toward our real desires and passions. Consider an aspiring public speaker, her coronary heart pounding as she stands in advance than a sea of faces. The fear she reports is not a signal to retreat, however a signal that she is stepping outside her comfort area, pursuing her passion, and tough herself to growth. By embracing worry as a compass, she navigates uncharted territories, discovering her voice and galvanizing others alongside the manner.

Fear and Personal Growth Growth lies on the alternative facet of worry, beckoning us to step into the unknown. Think of a shy introvert who desires of connecting with others thru public speaking. Fear grips her, tightening its hold as she envisions the judgment of others. But she recognizes that non-public increase lies beyond the bounds of her consolation place. With each speech she affords, fear retreats, changed by manner of self warranty and a newfound experience of empowerment. It is thru confronting fear that she unlocks her whole capacity and transforms proper right right into a charismatic communicator.

Fear as Fuel Fear has the power to ignite our internal fireside and fuel our determination. Imagine an athlete getting equipped for a excessive-stakes competition. Fear pulsates via their veins, however in preference to succumbing to its paralyzing grip, they channel it into their education habitual. The fear will become gasoline, pushing them to art work tougher, push their limits, and exceed their very personal expectancies. It is thru the crucible of fear that they emerge stronger, faster, and additional resilient.

Fear and Creativity, Fear can also be a muse, sparking creativity and innovation. Consider a author looking at a easy net net web page, fear whispering doubts approximately their functionality to weave phrases proper right

right into a fascinating story. Yet, it is through the concern of failure that they harness their imagination, crafting memories that captivate hearts and shipping readers to excellent worlds. Fear will become the catalyst for their creative expression, pushing them to discover new thoughts and push the limits in their craft.

Embracing Fear: The Hero's Journey In the hero's adventure, fear stands because the very last adversary to be confronted and conquered. It is the dragon guarding the treasure, the final obstacle on the path to self-attention. Heroes from historic myths to trendy legends encompass their fears, managing them head-on with unwavering strength of will. It is thru their fearless pursuit that they discover their true electricity and emerge effective, all the time changed through way in their adventure.

Dear adventurer, fear is not to be feared itself. It is a powerful pressure that would guide us, ignite our passions, and gasoline our private boom. By data the characteristic worry plays in our lives, we are able to remodel it from a trouble right into a stepping stone inside the route of greatness. So, allow us to step into the arena of worry with courage in our hearts, understanding that on the alternative aspect awaits the pleasure of unleashing our untapped potential and dwelling a life with out limits.

Identifying Fear-Based Patterns and Limiting Beliefs

In the massive tapestry of human lifestyles, fear frequently lurks in the shadows, wielding its have an impact on over our thoughts, feelings, and actions. It weaves complex patterns and plants seeds of doubt, maintaining us captive internal its grip. But what if we can also additionally want to decipher the code of fear, unraveling its elaborate patterns and figuring out the restricting ideals that hold us decrease lower returned? In this exciting excursion, we are capable of embark on a journey of self-discovery, as we unmask worry's illusions and unharness the strength inner us. With every step, we're capable of unveil the concern-based totally actually patterns that hinder our improvement and discover the transformative potential that lies dormant inner. So, equipment up and brace your self for an exciting journey into the depths of fear.

The Web of Fear Imagine a spider, spinning an complicated internet to ensnare its prey. Similarly, worry weaves its very very personal complex internet, trapping us in a cycle of self-doubt and limitations. We will find out the interconnected nature of fear-based totally certainly patterns, recognizing how one fear can supply starting to three exclusive, developing a tangled internet that restricts our boom.

The Power of Perception Perception is a effective lens through which we view the arena. Sometimes, our perceptions turn out to be distorted through worry, coloring our reviews and shaping our ideals. Picture a skilled artist who, due to a worry of criticism, hides their paintings away, in no manner allowing the area to understand their knowledge. By inspecting our perceptions and tough the ideals rooted in fear, we are able to damage unfastened from the chains that bind us.

Identifying Limiting Beliefs Limiting ideals are the shackles that preserve us once more, constraining our capability and stifling our goals. These ideals regularly arise from past opinions or societal conditioning, whispering messages of unworthiness and impossibility. Consider someone who goals of beginning their own corporation but believes they lack the essential abilities or assets. By figuring out the ones proscribing ideals, we are able to rewrite the narrative, changing doubt with empowerment and paving the manner for boom.

The Fear of Failure The worry of failure is a common thread that weaves its manner via our lives, dampening our spirits and halting our improvement. Yet, failure isn't always a verdict however a instructor, guiding us inside the course of fulfillment. Imagine an aspiring entrepreneur who, crippled through the priority of failure, stays caught in an unfulfilling task. By reframing failure as a stepping stone in choice to a stumbling block, we are able to break loose from its hold close and include the training it offers.

Escaping the Comparison Trap Comparison is a thief of delight, perpetuating the priority of no longer measuring as lots as others' achievements. It creates a in no way-finishing cycle of self-doubt and diminishes our self-worth. Envision a budding musician who, haunted thru the worry of no longer being as gifted as their friends, stifles their innovative expression. By spotting the futility of evaluation and celebrating our very very own specific adventure, we unlock ourselves from the restrictions it imposes.

Stepping into Vulnerability Fear frequently cloaks vulnerability in shadows, convincing us that it's miles a weakness to be avoided the least bit expenses. However, vulnerability is the birthplace of authenticity and connection. Picture a person yearning for deeper relationships but paralyzed with the aid of the use of the concern of rejection. By embracing vulnerability, we open ourselves as lots as considerable connections and create area for private growth and fulfillment.

Rewriting the Narrative The strength to rewrite our narrative lies inner us. We can venture the concern-primarily based patterns and restricting ideals that have held us captive and craft a cutting-edge tale of courage and empowerment. Consider an aspiring writer who, plagued via the concern of rejection, by no means stocks their paintings. By rewriting the narrative, they take the plunge, filing their manuscript and embracing the possibility of achievement.

Dear fearless adventurer, by means of the use of the usage of identifying worry-primarily based styles and limiting beliefs, we preserve the essential factor to unlocking our proper capability. As we resolve the complex internet of fear, we loose ourselves from its hold close to, allowing our genuine selves to polish. Let us embark in this interesting adventure of self-discovery, unmasking fear's illusions and unleashing the power inner. For it's miles in the face of fear that we find out the electricity, courage, and resilience wished to triumph over our barriers and step proper right into a existence filled with infinite possibilities.

Tools and Strategies for Overcoming Fear and Stepping Out of Comfort Zones

In the exhilarating tapestry of human lifestyles, fear regularly acts as an excellent barrier that continues us limited within the limits of our consolation zones. However, with the useful aid of harnessing the strength of transformative gear and techniques, we are able to smash loose from the shackles of fear and embark on a adventure of personal boom and success. In this empowering exploration, we can dive into real-existence examples and find the sensible techniques that permit humans to overcome worry and boldly step outside their comfort zones. So, gadget up and put together to equip your self with the gear essential to consist of exchange and unencumber your whole potential.

Mindset Shift: Embracing the Growth Mindset A vital first step in overcoming fear is cultivating a boom thoughts-set—a perception inside the capability to investigate, adapt, and beautify. By adopting this mind-set, individuals encompass stressful conditions as possibilities for growth in choice to obstacles to avoid. For example, endure in thoughts the story of a professional athlete who faces a modern-day, daunting competition. Instead of succumbing to worry, they technique it with a boom attitude, viewing it as a risk to decorate their skills and overall performance.

Visualization and Affirmations: Rewiring the Subconscious Visualization and affirmations are effective device that rewire the unconscious mind, permitting humans to overcome worry and step into new territory. For example, an aspiring public speaker may additionally additionally use visualization strategies to expect themselves turning in a captivating presentation with self belief and poise. By again and again setting beforehand their functionality, they create a terrific intellectual blueprint that strengthens their remedy and minimizes worry.

Gradual Exposure: The Power of Incremental Steps Taking incremental steps outside one's comfort area can be pretty effective in overcoming fear. This technique includes regularly exposing oneself to increasingly difficult situations. Take the instance of a person with a fear of heights. They can also moreover begin thru way of status on a sturdy balcony, then improvement to crossing a small bridge, and sooner or later overcome their worry via conducting sports like mountain climbing. Each step builds resilience and diminishes the priority related to the new experience.

Support Systems: Allies at the Journey Support structures play a vital function in presenting encouragement, steering, and obligation on the equal time as stepping out of consolation zones. Surrounding oneself with like-minded individuals who proportion similar aspirations creates a nurturing environment for non-public boom. For example, undergo in mind a budding entrepreneur who joins a agency mastermind organisation. The collective assist and shared critiques in the business enterprise offer precious insights, motivation, and a experience of camaraderie that bolsters their courage to take ambitious risks.

Embracing Failure: A Stepping Stone to Success Failure is an inevitable a part of boom and an possibility for beneficial mastering. Embracing failure as a teacher instead of a verdict can be freeing. Take the tale of a writer who gets multiple rejections for their manuscript. Instead of succumbing to melancholy, they view every rejection as a stepping stone, refining their craft and persisting until they robust a publishing deal. By reframing failure as a important a part of the journey, they in the end acquire success.

Mindfulness and Breathwork: Cultivating Inner Resilience Mindfulness and breathwork techniques provide people with the gadget to navigate worry and ache with grace and resilience. By grounding oneself in the gift 2d and regulating the breath, you likely can domesticate a experience of calm amidst tough situations. For instance, an character going through social tension can also exercising mindfulness and deep breathing bodily video games earlier than attending a networking event, letting them control their worry and engage with others with any luck.

Celebrating Progress: Fueling Motivation and Momentum Celebrating development, irrespective of how small, is important in maintaining motivation and sustaining momentum. Recognizing and acknowledging personal achievements boosts self-confidence and reinforces the perception that stepping out of the comfort area is a worthwhile agency. Whether it is completing a tough workout, handing over a a fulfillment presentation, or conquering a worry, celebrating the ones victories fuels the strength to keep embracing trade.

Dear courageous seeker, armed with those transformative equipment and strategies, you personal the potential to conquer worry and undertaking beyond the confines of your comfort vicinity. Real-existence examples illustrate the electricity of mind-set shifts, visualization, sluggish exposure, assist systems, embracing failure, mindfulness, and celebrating improvement. So, step boldly into the unknown, for it is there that you can discover your untapped capability, embody transformative increase, and forge a lifestyles packed with boundless opportunities.

Part II

Embracing New Life Chapters

Ahoy, fellow adventurer! Life's adventure is complete of twists and turns, and each new financial ruin brings with it thrilling possibilities and interesting escapades. In this exhilarating day adventure, we are able to dive headfirst into the arena of embracing new life chapters, all with a sprinkle of fun, laughter, and a zest for the unknown. So buckle up, placed in your adventurer's hat, and allow's embark on a pleasure-stuffed exploration of embracing the wondrous surprises that look ahead to us!

The Call to Adventure: Unveiling New Horizons Picture your self because the protagonist of your private epic story. The name to adventure beckons, and it's time to eliminate the anchors of the familiar. Embracing new existence chapters approach embracing the amusing of the unknown, like a fearless pirate setting sail for uncharted waters. Remember, lifestyles's maximum exhilarating moments are regularly located past the bounds of our consolation zones.

Embracing the Unpredictable: Dancing with Life's Twists and Turns Life's adventure is sort of a rollercoaster journey, full of sudden twists, turns, and loop-de-loops. Rather than clinging to reality, we can embody the satisfaction of the unpredictable. Just like a wild dance, we twirl and spin with each new financial disaster, allowing the rhythm of lifestyles to guide our steps. Who is aware of what adventures stay up for us spherical the subsequent nook?

The Magic of Beginner's Mind: Rediscovering Wonder In the hustle and bustle of day by day existence, it is easy to turn out to be jaded and lose sight of the wonder that surrounds us. Embracing new life chapters approach adopting the mind-set of a huge-eyed toddler, organized to find out and find out. From trying a modern-day-day hobby to immersing ourselves in a one in every of a kind manner of existence, drawing near every enjoy with a newbie's mind permits us to understand the magic and find out pride inside the handiest of factors.

Turning Fear into Fuel: Conquering Doubts and Leaping Forward Fear, that sneaky trickster, often attempts to maintain us lower again from embracing new studies. But what if we ought to reveal fear into gas? Imagine your self as a formidable superhero, going via your fears head-on and using them as stepping stones within the course of boom. Whether it is beginning a new profession, travelling solo, or pursuing a long-held dream, permit worry be the wind underneath your cape, propelling you to new heights.

Embracing Imperfections: Unleashing Your Authentic Self Perfectionism is the arch-nemesis of adventure and self-discovery. Embracing new existence chapters method embracing the splendor of imperfections, for they'll be what make us specific and right. Just like a unusual man or woman in a comedy film, we are able to snort at our mishaps and feature fun our quirks. By embracing our genuine selves, flaws and all, we unlock a international of self-popularity and proper connections.

A Crew of Kindred Spirits: Building Supportive Relationships No adventurer embarks on their journey by myself. Surrounding your self with a group of kindred spirits offers help, encouragement, and shared laughter along the manner. Just like a band of misfit pirates, your manual machine is conscious the united statesand downs of embracing new lifestyles chapters. They cheer you on, lend a helping hand, and percent inside the thrill of your triumphs. Together, you navigate the treacherous waters and function fun the hidden treasures you find out.

Living in the Present: Savoring Each Moment As we embark on new existence chapters, it's miles crucial to anchor ourselves in the present. Like a master yogi appearing a balancing act, we awareness on the proper right here and now, absolutely immersing ourselves in the richness of every second. From savoring a scrumptious meal to relishing the beauty of nature, embracing new reminiscences becomes a conscious exercise that deepens our appreciation for lifestyles's brilliant offers.

Dear intrepid explorer, the adventure of embracing new life chapters awaits you with open arms. It's a adventure complete of pleasure, growth, and infinite possibilities. So permit flow into of the mundane and dive into the first rate. Embrace the unknown, dance with the unpredictable, and unleash your proper self. With every step, go through in thoughts to cherish the winning and surround yourself with supportive souls who percentage within the pleasure. Your tale is unfolding, and the area eagerly awaits your subsequent financial ruin. Onward, with gusto and glee, to the interesting adventures that lies in advance!

Chapter 3: The Power Of Perspective
Shifting Your Mindset for New Beginnings

Step proper up, my fellow seekers of grand adventures and limitless potential! Prepare to embark on a mind-bending journey into the exhilarating realm of attitude—a amazing strain that might remodel even the best of beginnings into extraordinary opportunities. In this charming exploration, we are able to delve into the strength of transferring our attitude, igniting a spark of pride and surprise as we embody new beginnings with fervor and exuberance. So fasten your seatbelts and get organized to witness the breathtaking transformation that awaits!

Unveiling the Magic Lens: How Perspective Shapes Reality Imagine carrying a couple of magical spectacles that change the manner you understand the sector. Perspective acts as that enthralling lens, changing our truth and unveiling hidden possibilities. Just like an illusionist performing enthralling guidelines, transferring our mind-set well-known glowing angles, unexplored paths, and untapped functionality in the mundane. Through this lens, even the smallest seed of a new starting can bloom proper proper right into a extraordinary tapestry of boom and success.

The Mindset Metamorphosis: Embracing Growth and Learning Embarking on new beginnings necessitates a transformative mindset—one which embraces boom and sees disturbing conditions as stepping stones to fulfillment. Imagine your self as a budding butterfly, breaking free from the restrictions of your vintage techniques. By embracing a thoughts-set of non-stop analyzing and personal development, you unfold your wings and gracefully jump into uncharted territory, organized to triumph over new heights.

From Obstacles to Opportunities: Flipping the Script In the theater of lifestyles, boundaries frequently take center degree, threatening to hose down our spirits and thwart our improvement. But what if we need to rewrite the script? Shifting our thoughts-set permits us to view boundaries as possibilities in cover. Just like a professional improviser, we adapt and turn unexpected challenges into moments of increase and innovation. It's thru those apparently insurmountable hurdles that we discover our resilience and discover hidden strengths.

The Power of Gratitude: Finding Joy in Every Beginning Gratitude, that colourful elixir of the soul, has the power to transform our angle on new beginnings. Like a superb fireworks show, working towards gratitude illuminates the splendor and abundance present in each second. By shifting our recognition from what's missing to what we already have, we infuse our beginnings with satisfaction and appreciation. With each step forward, we have a good time the adventure, spotting the advantages that surround us.

Embracing Change: Dancing with Uncertainty Change, like a mischievous dancer, sweeps us off our ft and twirls us into the unknown. Yet, by using the usage of shifting our angle, we are capable of come to be swish companions in this hard dance. Rather than fearing change, we discover ways to consist of it as a catalyst for boom and discovery. Like a seasoned dancer, we adapt our steps to the rhythm of uncertainty, trusting that every new beginning holds inner it the seeds of transformation.

Reinventing Identity: Embracing the Multifaceted Self As we project into new beginnings, we've got the notable opportunity to reinvent ourselves—to discover the big depths of our multifaceted identities. Like a draw near artist with a colorful palette, we can paint ourselves anew, incorporating new passions, skills, and studies into the tapestry of our lives. Shifting our mind-set lets in us to break unfastened from the confines of self-imposed boundaries and encompass the ever-evolving nature of our being.

Collaboration and Connection: Amplifying New Beginnings New beginnings are not solitary endeavors however trips shared with fellow adventurers. By shifting our mind-set to simply considered considered one of collaboration and connection, we open ourselves as a fantastic deal as a international of help, concept, and shared victories. Just like a symphony orchestra, each tool performs a very precise function in developing a harmonious melody. Through collaboration, we make bigger the effect of our new beginnings, growing a symphony of transformation and collective growth.

Dear fearless explorer of the mind, you currently possess the call of the sport key to liberate the exhilarating power of attitude.

Through this adventure, we've determined how angle shapes our truth, transforms limitations into possibilities, and infuses new beginnings with gratitude, adaptability, and connection. With each new monetary wreck, consider to don your magical lens, embracing the kaleidoscope of possibilities that lie earlier than you. The degree is about, the place eagerly awaits your grand standard typical overall performance—so jump ahead with pleasure, interest, and the unwavering notion that every new beginning holds the potential for exquisite adventures. Onward, courageous soul, to the breathtaking landscapes that look beforehand in your exploration.

Cultivating a Growth Mindset: Embracing a Positive Outlook

Welcome, fellow adventurers of the mind, to a exquisite adventure into the arena of the growth thoughts-set—a place wherein opportunities are as big due to the fact the celebs inside the sky and wherein a excellent outlook propels us to new heights of personal and professional boom. In this charming exploration, we can embark on a pride-stuffed quest to cultivate a boom mind-set, all at the same time as embracing the playful spirit internal us. So, buckle up, positioned to your imagination cap, and allow's embark on a a laugh-crammed journey into the sector of boundless functionality!

The Mindset Metropolis: Where Dreams Take Flight Imagine a bustling town wherein goals come alive—a place wherein skyscrapers of possibility tower over the streets of creativeness. Cultivating a increase mind-set method turning into a resident of this staggering city, wherein positivity and optimism lay the foundation for limitless boom. In this colorful realm, worrying situations are seen as possibilities for growth, screw ups are stepping stones to success, and setbacks are simply detours on the path to greatness.

The Power of Yet: The Magical Word of Possibility In the growth mindset u . S . A ., the phrase "but" possesses a magical great. When faced with a undertaking or a talent but to be mastered, definitely consisting of "but" at the give up of a sentence opens the door to a international of possibility. "I have not located it... Yet." "I can not do it... But." This tiny phrase holds the vital factor to unlocking our functionality, transforming perceived barriers into stepping stones on our journey of growth. Embracing the strength of but invitations us to encompass the joy of studying and the delight of what lies ahead.

The Adventure of "Not Yet": Celebrating the Journey In our growth mind-set excursion, we apprehend that fulfillment is not measured definitely by means of the vacation spot however through the adventures alongside the way. Each leap in advance, every stumble, and every triumph will become part of our precise tale. Just like intrepid explorers, we have got amusing the journey, savoring the thrill of development and relishing the schooling determined. It's the technique of boom that brings us success, and every "now not but" second becomes an interesting chapter in our ever-evolving story.

The Playful Potion: Learning through Curiosity In the growth attitude realm, interest reigns first-rate. It's the playful potion that fuels our preference to find out, discover, and have a look at. Like a mischievous sprite, hobby invitations us to invite questions, are looking for new evaluations, and approach disturbing conditions with a revel in of marvel. It transforms the normal into the incredible, infusing our journey with pleasure and delight. With interest as our guide, we launch the door to countless opportunities, making getting to know a thrilling journey.

From Limits to Superpowers: Embracing the "Can-Do" Attitude In the boom attitude universe, we shed the cloak of self-imposed barriers and include our internal superheroes. We replace thoughts of "I cannot" with the resounding refrain of "I can." Like caped crusaders, we tap into our particular strengths, competencies, and talents, unleashing them to address challenges head-on. This "can-do" mind-set will become our superpower, propelling us to conquer limitations, accomplish splendid feats, and encourage others to do the equal.

The Party of Persistence: Dancing with Determination Persistence is the lifestyles of the increase thoughts-set celebration—a energetic celebration in which setbacks are met with resilience, and determination is the dance companion that in no manner we have to us falter. Like energetic dancers, we persevere through challenges, studying from each misstep and moving within the path of our dreams. We recognize that success isn't always on the spot however a cease cease result of constant try and unwavering belief. So, let's positioned on our dancing footwear and waltz via the limitations, knowledge that every leap forward brings us towards our dreams.

Spreading the Growth Magic: Inspiring Others As we domesticate a growth attitude, we come to be ambassadors of opportunity, spreading the mystical energy of boom to those round us. By embodying a splendid outlook, we encourage others to encompass their non-public trips of boom and unharness their endless ability. Like enthusiastic magicians, we percent our guidelines of resilience, optimism, and perseverance, igniting sparks of increase in every heart we contact.

Dear adventurers of the boom thoughts-set, as we end our whimsical day experience, permit's carry the spirit of positivity and playfulness with us on our ongoing quest for personal and expert boom. Remember, the boom thoughts-set realm is an area of boundless potential, in which worrying situations grow to be adventures and setbacks transform into stepping stones. So, allow's hold our adventure with delight, hobby, and the unwavering notion that we are capable of splendid changes. Onward we bypass, weaving a tapestry of growth and embracing the power of a playful mindset!

Embracing Uncertainty: Finding Opportunity in Change

Welcome, courageous souls, to a interesting day journey into the uncharted territories of uncertainty—an interesting realm in which exchange reigns brilliant and opportunities abound. In this exhilarating exploration, we will embark on a journey to find out the hidden treasures that lie inside the unknown. So fasten your seatbelts, for we are approximately to delve into the pleasure of embracing uncertainty and coming across the infinite opportunities that look ahead to!

Embracing the Dance of Change Life is a grand dance ground, and alternate is the rhythm that actions us earlier. Embracing uncertainty is like stepping onto that dance floor with pleasure and anticipation, organized to twirl, bounce, and spin in sync with the ever-evolving song of life. Just as a professional dancer adjusts their steps to the changing pace, we too discover ways to adapt and discover our footing amidst uncertainty, coming across the beauty and thrill that lie inside each new skip.

The Magic of Serendipity: Unexpected Discoveries In the significant tapestry of uncertainty, serendipity turns into our guiding celeb, foremost us to surprising encounters and beautiful discoveries. Embracing the unknown opens the door to chance encounters, fortuitous sports, and splendid synchronicities that add spice and satisfaction to our journey. Like treasure hunters, we assignment into uncharted waters, trusting that serendipity will unveil precious gems alongside the way.

Cultivating a Resilient Spirit: Thriving Amidst Change Uncertainty can be an intimidating pressure, but indoors it lies the possibility to domesticate a resilient spirit. Like strong alrighttrees that resist storms, we also can extend the electricity and flexibility to thrive amidst trade. Embracing uncertainty allows us to tap into our internal resilience, adaptability, and resourcefulness. With each assignment we conquer, we emerge stronger and extra assured, organized to conquer new frontiers.

Unlocking Creativity: Thinking Outside the Box In the place of uncertainty, creativity turns into a trusted partner, empowering us to anticipate beyond the boundaries of the known. When confronted with alternate, we unleash our creativeness and tap into our progressive reservoirs, discovering innovative solutions and glowing views. Like bold inventors, we push the boundaries, defy conventions, and embody the satisfaction of coming across new and unexplored opportunities.

From Fear to Freedom: Liberating the Mind Uncertainty often breeds worry, as our minds grapple with the unknown and the ability dangers that lie earlier. However, in embracing uncertainty, we've got the electricity to transform worry into freedom. We undertaking the restrictions imposed thru way of our non-public thoughts, releasing ourselves from the shackles of fear and tension. Like intrepid explorers, we soar forward with courage, emboldened thru using the belief that inner uncertainty lies the route to increase and private liberation.

Opportunity Amidst Chaos: Finding the Silver Lining In the whirlwind of uncertainty, chaos may additionally seem to reign. Yet, inside chaos lies hidden possibility—a shimmering silver lining equipped to be located. Embracing uncertainty allows us to view disruptions as catalysts for super change, to perceive the openings amidst the turmoil, and to seize the possibilities that upward push up. Like skillful surfers, we journey the waves of uncertainty, harnessing their strength to propel us inside the course of unimagined beaches of achievement.

The Adventure of Self-Discovery: Unveiling New Horizons Embracing uncertainty is not surely a adventure outward but additionally a journey inward—an adventure of self-discovery and private growth. In the face of trade, we confront our fears, question our assumptions, and peel returned the layers of self-imposed obstacles. We discover hidden strengths, passions, and aspirations that would were dormant within us. Like intrepid explorers of the soul, we bravely task into the unexplored realms of our being, uncovering new horizons of cause and fulfillment.

Dear adventurers of uncertainty, as we finish our exciting excursion, permit us to deliver with us the spirit of exhilaration and possibility. Embracing uncertainty unveils a international of serendipity, resilience, creativity, and possibility. It empowers us to triumph over worry, discover hidden treasures, and embark on a voyage of self-discovery. So, allow us to embody the a laugh of alternate, dance to the rhythm of uncertainty, and free up the infinite ability that awaits us. Onward we flow into, fearlessly embracing the unknown, and alluring the exhilarating adventure of embracing uncertainty!

Harnessing Resilience: Bouncing Back from Setbacks and Challenges

Welcome, courageous souls, to a transformative adventure into the region of resilience—an area wherein setbacks and demanding situations are met with unwavering energy of will and an indomitable spirit. In this motivational exploration, we will delve into the art work of harnessing resilience, unlocking the power inner us to get better from adversity and embody a lifestyles of countless possibilities. So, gather your strength, ignite your inner fireside, and permit us to embark on a transformative journey of resilience and triumph!

Embracing the Power Within Resilience is the catalyst that propels us beforehand, even within the face of adversity. It is the the usage of pressure that permits us to navigate the stormy seas of existence with courage and tenacity. In this bankruptcy, we're capable of discover the transformative strength of resilience and consist of the perception that every body very own the internal power to triumph over demanding situations and emerge more potent than ever earlier than.

Thriving inside the Face of Setbacks Resilience starts offevolved with our thoughts-set—a mind-set that sees setbacks as opportunities for increase and analyzing. By moving our mind-set, we remodel boundaries into stepping stones, failures into valuable training, and adversity into gasoline for private and expert improvement. In this bankruptcy, we can find out the secrets and strategies of cultivating a resilient thoughts-set and discover the manner it empowers us to thrive amidst life's disturbing situations.

Strengthening Our Inner Core Just like physical exercise builds our muscle businesses, intentional efforts should make stronger our resilience muscular tissues. Through intentional exercise, we growth the functionality to evolve, persevere, and get over setbacks. We will discover practical strategies together with self-care, cultivating a help network, and fostering a increase-oriented attitude that nourishes our resilience muscle groups and permits us to get higher with unwavering electricity.

Finding Silver Linings Adversity is a powerful instructor, offering profitable schooling that shape our man or woman and pork up our resilience. In this financial disaster, we are able to explore the manner to embody the lessons hidden inner adversity, uncovering the silver linings that emerge from difficult situations. We will discover how resilience allows us redecorate setbacks into opportunities, paving the manner for personal boom and a renewed revel in of motive.

Turning Obstacles into Triumphs Resilience and perseverance flow into hand in hand, like a symphony gambling a a success melody. When confronted with boundaries, we tap into our reservoirs of resilience, summoning the braveness to persevere and overcome. Through inspiring examples from actual-existence heroes, we're capable of witness the transformative electricity of perseverance, demonstrating that with unwavering strength of mind, we're in a position to turn even the most difficult times into brilliant triumphs.

Nurturing Supportive Networks Resilience thrives in the commercial agency corporation of supportive relationships. In this chapter, we're able to discover the power of connection and the manner nurturing resilient relationships can bolster our potential to bounce back from setbacks. We will find out the pride and strength that comes from sharing our journey with compassionate pals, mentors, and cherished ones who provide encouragement, guidance, and a strong space for us to expand and heal.

Thriving in Life's Dance Resilience isn't always a holiday spot however a way of existence—a dance we perform with grace and backbone. In this very last chapter, we can combine the training we have got found and embody the spirit of resilience as a lifelong workout. We will rejoice the moments of triumph, widely recognized the growth that emerges from adversity, and commit ourselves to a existence of resilience, braveness, and unwavering perseverance.

Dear resilient souls, as we quit this empowering adventure, let us supply the flame of resilience within us, understanding that setbacks and demanding situations are not roadblocks but opportunities for growth. With unwavering strength of mind, we are able to bounce back from any setback, embody the instructions of adversity, and create a existence of triumph and achievement. So, let us dance with resilience, unleash our inner electricity, and light up the route with our indomitable spirit. Onward we pass, resilient and unstoppable, equipped to encompass life's stressful situations and overcome them with unwavering electricity!

Chapter 4: Navigating Transitions

Strategies for Successfully Transitioning to New Life Chapters

Life is a chain of transitions, a never-ending journey of latest beginnings and chapters geared up to be written. Navigating these transitions with grace and resilience is a capacity actually really worth analyzing. In this insightful exploration, we will embark on a voyage of discovery, uncovering strategies to efficaciously navigate transitions and encompass the limitless possibilities that lie in advance. So, hoist the sails, consistent the compass, and allow us to set forth on a transformative adventure of transitioning to new life chapters.

Change is the wind that fills our sails, propelling us within the course of latest horizons. In this chapter, we can find out the significance of embracing alternate and the mind-set had to navigate transitions effectively. We will discover ways to recognize the signs and symptoms that propose the need for a transition and embody the winds of change as opportunities for growth and transformation.

Setting Goals and Creating a Vision Before embarking on any adventure, it's far important to have a clean vacation spot in thoughts. In this financial disaster, we can delve into the device of putting dreams and developing a vision for the ultra-modern lifestyles monetary disaster in advance. We will find out realistic techniques for outlining our aspirations, mapping out a roadmap, and installing location milestones to guide us through the transition.

Building Resilience and Support Just as a sailor prepares their vessel earlier than placing sail, we too have to put together ourselves for the journey of transition. In this financial disaster, we're able to discover techniques for building resilience, nurturing self-care practices, and cultivating a resource network. We will find out how those pillars of strength offer us with the stableness and fortitude needed to navigate the demanding situations and uncertainties of transitions.

Release and Renewal Transitioning to a modern-day-day lifestyles financial ruin calls for letting move of the familiar. In this bankruptcy, we're able to discover the paintings of release and renewal, letting bypass of attachments to the beyond and embracing the possibilities of the prevailing 2d. We will discover ways to emerge as aware about and launch limiting ideals, old patterns, and emotional baggage, growing space for emblem spanking new evaluations and growth.

Cultivating a Growth Mindset Transitions regularly involve stepping into the unknown, and a growth mindset becomes our compass, guiding us thru uncharted waters. In this monetary catastrophe, we are able to find out the strength of a increase thoughts-set, cultivating interest, adaptability, and a willingness to check. We will discover how embracing the unknown opens doorways to new possibilities, expands our abilities, and ignites our experience of journey.

Overcoming Challenges and Resilience No journey is without demanding conditions, and transitions aren't any exception. In this financial catastrophe, we can find out techniques for overcoming boundaries and building resilience in the course of instances of alternate. We will discover ways to navigate hard seas, keep a outstanding mind-set, and extend trouble-solving abilties that allow us to live on course, regardless of the disturbing situations we stumble upon.

Acknowledging Growth and Progres As we sail via transitions, it is important to have a laugh the milestones alongside the way. In this financial ruin, we're capable of discover the importance of acknowledging our growth and development, spotting the small victories that lead us inside the path of our preferred destination. We will learn how to recognize the adventure itself, locating pleasure in the technique of transitioning and embracing the changes that spread.

Dear navigators of transitions, as we attain the prevent of this transformative journey, allow us to deliver with us the data and techniques had to sail easily into new existence chapters. Transitions aren't to be feared however embraced as possibilities for boom, self-discovery, and private fulfillment. So, let us set sail with self guarantee, navigate with resilience, and encompass the winds of alternate that propel us within the course of a future complete of limitless possibilities. Bon voyage, my fellow adventurers, as you navigate transitions and embark on new existence chapters with grace, resilience, and a sense of satisfaction!

Preparing for Change: Planning and Setting Intentions

Change is a powerful pressure that sweeps through our lives, beckoning us to increase, evolve, and encompass new opportunities. In this exhilarating adventure, we're capable of find out the artwork of creating geared up for change, igniting the fireplace internal us to chart a path inside the path of our favored future. Buckle up, luxurious adventurers, as we embark on a interesting exploration of making plans and placing intentions, propelling us in the direction of a destiny entire of excitement, cause, and achievement.

Embracing the Call for Change: Change is a name to rouse the dormant dreams, passions, and desires inside us. In this financial ruin, we're capable of ignite the spark of delight and interest for the transformative journey in advance. We will discover the reasons why trade is crucial, the way it opens doors to new opportunities, and the methods wherein it expands our horizons. Let us encompass the choice for trade with open hearts and a willingness to embark on a interesting journey.

Unveiling the Power of Planning: Planning is the compass that guides us via the ever-converting panorama of life. In this monetary damage, we will discover the art of powerful planning, outlining our desires, and mapping out the steps had to collect them. We will find out the importance of putting clear targets, developing actionable plans, and breaking them down into plausible obligations. Let us harness the electricity of making plans to deliver our desires to life.

Setting Intentions: Igniting the Inner Fire Intentions are the fuel that propels us in advance, infusing our actions with cause and ardour. In this monetary disaster, we are able to delve into the method of placing intentions, aligning our thoughts, feelings, and movements with our favored outcomes. We will discover the electricity of purpose to create a powerful mind-set, domesticate motivation, and ignite the hearth internal us. Let us set intentions that inspire us and guide us in the path of the change we trying to find.

Crafting a Vision: Painting a Vivid Future A imaginative and prescient is the masterpiece we paint with our imagination, shaping the truth we want to create. In this bankruptcy, we're capable of find out the art of crafting a compelling vision for the destiny. We will learn how to tap into our creativity, visualize our desired results, and imbue our imaginative and prescient with vibrant information. Let us create a imaginative and prescient that excites us, fuels our passion, and serves as a guiding mild on our adventure of change.

Overcoming Obstacles: Building Resilience and Adaptability Change regularly brings obstacles along the way, trying out our resilience and flexibility. In this bankruptcy, we will discover techniques for overcoming boundaries, building resilience, and embracing the energy of adaptability. We will find out the mindset needed to navigate worrying situations, broaden trouble-solving abilities, and keep a exceptional outlook. Let us encompass trade's unpredictable nature and rise above any barriers that come our manner.

Embracing the Growth Mindset: Expanding Our Capacities A growth mind-set is the fertile soil wherein trade prospers. In this bankruptcy, we are capable of delve into the energy of a increase mind-set, fostering a belief in our potential to look at, develop, and adapt. We will explore the significance of embracing demanding conditions, searching for new tales, and embracing non-stop learning. Let us domesticate a thoughts-set that sees change as an opportunity for increase and personal transformation.

Taking Action: Igniting the Spark of Change Change requires movement, for it is through motion that our intentions come to existence. In this economic damage, we are capable of discover the importance of taking regular and practical motion to show up our preferred modifications. We will have a look at to overcome procrastination, assemble conduct that useful resource our desires, and live advocated along the way. Let us ignite the spark of change within us and step boldly into the motion required to deliver our visions to fruition.

Dear adventurers of alternate, as we achieve the stop of this invigorating journey, allow us to carry the fireplace of training inner us, prepared to embody the winds of change with enthusiasm and determination. By embracing the selection for change, setting intentions, crafting a compelling imaginative and prescient, overcoming obstacles, cultivating a increase thoughts-set, and taking functional motion, we are geared up to embark on a terrific adventure of transformation. So, ignite the fireside indoors you, highly-priced explorers, and allow the journey of making geared up for change be an exciting and worthwhile path closer to a destiny packed with pleasure, cause, and countless possibilities.

Building a Support System: Finding and Cultivating a Network

Life is a grand journey, fine embarked upon with a network of useful useful resource via using our element. In this exhilarating exploration, we will delve into the art work of constructing a useful resource tool, weaving a web of connection that uplifts, conjures up, and empowers us on our adventure. So, accumulate your enthusiasm and be part of me as we find the secrets to finding and cultivating a community that fuels our delight and propels us to new heights.

The Power of Connection: Connection is the thread that weaves the material of our lives together. In this financial disaster, we are capable of dive into the profound impact of human connection on our well-being and private boom. We will find out the methods wherein a assist tool can provide us with encouragement, steering, and a enjoy of belonging. Let us include the electricity of connection and understand its potential to mild up our lives.

Identifying Your Needs and Desires: Before embarking on the journey of building a assist machine, it's miles crucial to discover our goals and goals. In this financial ruin, we can interact in self-meditated photo and introspection, gaining readability at the sorts of assist we're searching out. Whether it is emotional help, expert steering, or a shared enjoy of purpose, allow us to understand our particular desires and lay the foundation for a guide device that fulfills them.

Seeking Kindred Spirits: Kindred spirits are the gas that ignites our passion and elevates our journey. In this financial disaster, we are able to find out strategies for locating like-minded people who percentage our hobbies, values, and aspirations. We will find out the significance of seeking out businesses, companies, and social groups that align with our passions. Let us cast our net massive and invite kindred spirits into our lives.

Cultivating Meaningful Relationships: Building a manual device is going beyond mere acquaintanceship; it thrives on significant relationships. In this monetary damage, we will discover the secrets and techniques and techniques to cultivating deep and right connections with the ones in our assist network. We will discover powerful verbal exchange, active listening, and the artwork of vulnerability. Let us nurture relationships that stand the check of time and weather the storms of existence.

Mentorship and Guidance: Mentors are the guiding lighting that take away darkness from our direction to achievement. In this bankruptcy, we're able to find out the power of mentorship and are looking for for out individuals who can offer us with guidance, know-how, and information. We will explore the art of finding mentors, nurturing the ones relationships, and making the most of their valuable insights. Let us are on the lookout for for out mentors who encourage us to reach for the celebs.

The synergy of collaboration can take us to improbable heights. In this financial disaster, we're capable of find out the strength of collaborative opportunities inner our guide tool. We will discover the pleasure of working collectively, sharing belongings, and co-growing extensive opinions. Let us tap into the collective information and creativity of our help community, unlocking the capacity for exponential boom.

Nurturing and Giving Back Building a assist tool is a -manner road. In this monetary disaster, we're able to examine the paintings of nurturing and giving again to our network. We will explore processes to offer assist, encouragement, and thought to those round us. Let us create a way of life of reciprocity, in which we uplift every different and foster an environment of non-prevent increase and manual.

Dear champions of connection, as we conclude this thrilling journey of building a resource device, allow us to carry the knowledge and notion inside us to weave a web of connection that uplifts and empowers us. By embracing the energy of connection, identifying our goals, looking for kindred spirits, cultivating massive relationships, embracing mentorship, taking component, and nurturing our network, we create a manual device that propels us ahead on our grand journey. So, allow us to embark in this thrilling quest, costly explorers, and can the connections we forge mild our manner to a destiny complete of excitement, boom, and boundless possibilities.

Managing Change: Adapting and Adjusting to New Circumstances

Change is the rhythm of lifestyles, and our ability to navigate its twists and turns determines our success and success. In this transformative journey, we are able to delve into the paintings of dealing with exchange, reading to conform and alter to new instances with grace and resilience. Together, permit's find out actual-lifestyles examples that illustrate the energy of version and find out the strategies that allow us to encompass the dance of trade.

Embracing the Fluid Nature of Change: Change is a ordinary partner on our adventure, requiring us to embody its fluidity. In this financial disaster, we can delve into the information that change is inevitable and essential for growth. We will discover real-existence examples of humans who've efficiently tailored to new conditions, highlighting the significance of flexibility and open-mindedness. Let us learn how to enjoy the waves of trade and find out the possibilities that lie within its currents.

Developing a Growth Mindset: A boom mind-set is the crucial detail to unlocking our capability for model. In this monetary catastrophe, we are capable of explore actual-life stories of human beings who have embraced a increase attitude, demonstrating the power of resilience and a amazing outlook. We will discover ways to shift our mind-set, view challenges as possibilities for increase, and cultivate a mind-set that flourishes on alternate. Let us harness the transformative electricity of a growth attitude to navigate the ever-converting landscape of lifestyles.

Building Resilience within the Face of Change: Resilience is the armor that protects us within the course of times of alternate. In this financial catastrophe, we can examine actual-life examples of people who have exhibited super resilience within the face of adversity. We will discover the techniques they hired to get higher, adapt, and thrive. Let us draw concept from their memories and find out the inner power had to navigate uncertain times.

Adapting to New Environments and Cultures: Change often entails adjusting to new environments and cultures. In this chapter, we will find out real-lifestyles examples of humans who've embraced new environment, highlighting the energy of adaptability and cultural intelligence. We will look at from their studies, coming across the importance of hobby, empathy, and a willingness to study from others. Let us amplify our horizons and feature a laugh the richness of range that change brings.

Navigating Career Transitions: Career transitions present unique stressful conditions and possibilities for boom. In this chapter, we are able to discover actual-life memories of people who have efficiently navigated profession modifications, showcasing the significance of resilience, self-mirrored photograph, and adaptableness. We will research the way they leveraged their abilties, embraced new possibilities, and redefined their professional paths. Let us gather notion from their trips and embody the possibilities that career transitions offer.

Adapting to Technological Advances: Technological upgrades have revolutionized our international, requiring us to evolve and embody new tool and tactics of strolling. In this bankruptcy, we can find out real-life examples of human beings who have embraced technological trade, highlighting the importance of interest, non-forestall mastering, and versatility. We will witness how they harnessed the strength of generation to decorate their lives and careers. Let us include technological development and capture the possibilities it presents.

Nurturing Self-Care and Emotional Well-being: Managing trade requires looking after our emotional well-being. In this chapter, we can explore real-existence memories of individuals who have prioritized self-care inside the route of instances of exchange, showcasing the significance of mindfulness, self-compassion, and in search of guide. We will discover how they nurtured their emotional nicely-being, fostering resilience and adaptableness. Let us make self-care a state of affairs as we navigate the ebb and glide of change.

As we finish this transformative exploration of coping with trade, allow us to deliver with us the information and perception gained from actual-existence examples. By embracing the fluid nature of change, developing a increase mindset, constructing resilience, adapting to new environments, navigating career transitions, embracing technological advances, and nurturing self-care, we empower ourselves to bounce with trade gracefully. So, allow us to embark in this exhilarating journey, luxurious adventurers, and encompass the rhythm of version with self assurance and joy.

Part III

Embracing Challenges and Achieving Growth

Welcome to the exhilarating finale of our adventure, in which we dive into the transformative electricity of embracing traumatic situations and accomplishing private boom. In this exciting financial spoil, we are capable of find out actual-lifestyles case research that exemplify the awesome heights we will obtain at the same time as we're going through adversity head-on. So, buckle up, high priced explorers, as we embark on a journey complete of exhilaration, idea, and boundless possibilities for growth.

Case Study: John's Journey from Failure to Triumph

Meet John, a decided entrepreneur who faced numerous setbacks on his direction to success. In this chapter, we are able to witness John's resilience in movement as he navigates thru disasters, monetary struggles, and fierce opposition. We will explore the mind-set and strategies that allowed him to get higher, adapt his method, and in the long run gain his dreams. John's adventure serves as a powerful reminder of the indomitable human spirit and the transformative strength of resilience.

Case Study: Sarah's Leap of Faith

Sarah, a timid introvert, embarks on a life-converting adventure via stepping out of doors her comfort place. In this chapter, we may be part of Sarah as she takes up public speaking, travels solo, and embraces new evaluations that undertaking her fears and obstacles. We will witness her personal increase, extended self belief, and advanced horizons as she confronts the unknown with braveness and interest. Sarah's story inspires us to push past our consolation zones and discover the untapped functionality that lies interior.

Case Study: Alex's Journey via Adversity

Alex, a passionate artist, faces a devastating damage that during quick robs him of his capability to create. In this monetary destroy, we are capable of witness Alex's journey of transformation as he harnesses the power of a growth thoughts-set. We will find out how he embraces opportunity creative expressions, learns new strategies, and in the long run turns his adversity into an opportunity for innovative exploration and innovation. Alex's tale illustrates the notable energy of thoughts-set in overcoming demanding situations and locating new paths to success.

Case Study: Emma's Pursuit of Excellence

Emma, an aspiring athlete, reviews repeated disasters and setbacks on her quest for mastery. In this bankruptcy, we're capable of have a look at Emma's adventure as she embraces failure as a stepping stone to success. We will witness her resilience, location, and unwavering willpower to improvement as she learns from her mistakes, seeks remarks, and always refines her capabilities. Emma's story teaches us that failure isn't the give up however an essential part of the journey in the path of excellence.

Case Study: David's Career Transition

David, a seasoned expert, finds himself at a crossroads in his career. In this financial ruin, we're able to accompany David as he navigates the uncertainties of a career transition. We will discover how he embraces exchange, hones new competencies, and adapts to a hastily evolving company. David's story highlights the importance of embracing trade, seizing new possibilities, and harnessing one's specific strengths to thrive in an ever-converting international.

Case Study: Maya's Mentorship Journey

Maya, a greater youthful entrepreneur, embarks on a mentorship journey that transforms her employer and personal increase. In this economic smash, we are capable of witness the transformative strength of mentorship as Maya seeks steerage from a pro organisation chief. We will find out how the mentor's knowledge, useful resource, and steerage propel Maya to new heights of success and self-discovery. Maya's adventure reminds us of the profound impact mentorship might also need to have on our journey towards non-public and expert boom.

As we finish this exhilarating exploration of embracing annoying conditions and accomplishing non-public increase, the training from our fascinating case research resonate deeply inner us. We have witnessed the energy of resilience, stepping outside our comfort zones, embracing the unknown, turning adversity into possibility, mastering from failure, and the value of mentorship. Now, armed with notion and insights, allow us to fearlessly consist of demanding situations, push our obstacles, and free up our actual capability. Together, allow us to embark on a lifelong adventure of growth, delight, and infinite opportunities.

Chapter 5: Strategies For Overcoming Obstacles

Life is a tapestry of disturbing conditions, and our capacity to face them head-on defines our man or woman and shapes our future. In this transformative adventure, we will find out the strategies and attitude wished to triumph over limitations with resilience and backbone. Through real-existence examples, we're able to witness the strength of human spirit and find out how humans have conquered adversity. So, allow us to embark in this inspiring adventure, high priced adventurers, and discover ways to navigate the route of triumph.

The Foundation for Success Case Study: Thomas Edison and the Invention of the Light Bulb

Thomas Edison, the famend inventor, confronted endless failures and setbacks on his path to inventing the slight bulb. In this chapter, we're capable of delve into Edison's unwavering notion in his abilties and his dedication to studying from every setback. We will discover how his growth thoughts-set allowed him to persist regardless of boundaries and ultimately acquire massive success. Edison's story serves as a effective reminder of the importance of embracing stressful conditions as possibilities for growth.

Turning Obstacles into Opportunities Case Study: Elon Musk and the SpaceX Journey

Elon Musk, the visionary entrepreneur, encountered numerous demanding conditions in his quest to revolutionize place exploration with SpaceX. In this financial ruin, we're capable of delve into Musk's trouble-fixing mind-set and his capacity to show boundaries into possibilities. We will discover how he tackled technical problems, financial constraints, and industry skepticism with innovative solutions and an unwavering perception in his imaginative and prescient. Musk's story demonstrates the power of a trouble-solving mind-set in overcoming annoying situations and conducting superb desires.

The Strength of Community Case Study: The Miracle on the Hudson - Captain Chesley "Sully" Sullenberger

Captain Sully Sullenberger, the hero pilot who efficaciously landed US Airways Flight 1549 at the Hudson River, confronted a existence-or-dying state of affairs with restricted time for choice-making. In this economic catastrophe, we're capable of witness the essential role of a robust aid community in overcoming disturbing conditions. We will find out how Captain Sully's knowledge, teamwork, and the assist of his crew and air web site visitors controllers contributed to the a fulfillment final consequences. His story emphasizes the importance of looking for assist, constructing sturdy relationships, and counting on others all through hard times.

Thriving in a Changing Landscape Case Study: Netflix and the Evolution of Streaming

Netflix, the worldwide streaming huge, confronted numerous worrying conditions in its evolution from a DVD-thru way of-mail company to a digital streaming platform. In this economic disaster, we are able to delve into Netflix's functionality to comply and innovate inside the face of converting purchaser alternatives and technological improvements. We will find out how the enterprise agency embraced new technology, experimented with content material material, and disrupted the conventional entertainment enterprise. The Netflix case test exemplifies the importance of adaptability, innovation, and willingness to include exchange.

Key to Overcoming Obstacles Case Study: J.K. Rowling and the Harry Potter Series

J.K. Rowling, the writer of the immensely famous Harry Potter collection, faced severa rejections and private hardships on her adventure to success. In this monetary catastrophe, we are able to find out Rowling's relentless endurance and unwavering willpower to supply her magical international to life. We will delve into her journey of self-notion, creativity, and resilience, which subsequently precipitated the creation of one of the maximum loved literary franchises of all time. Rowling's story is a testament to the electricity of staying energy and determination in overcoming barriers and carrying out greatness.

As we end this superb exploration of going via worrying situations head-on, we're stimulated with the aid of the use of the memories of people who have overcome seemingly insurmountable boundaries. Through their resilience, hassle-solving thoughts-set, assist networks, adaptability, and sheer dedication, they have got verified that no impediment is just too exquisite to triumph over. Let us embody those strategies in our very very own lives, costly adventurers, and face challenges with courage, tenacity, and a steadfast notion in our capability to overcome. With each impediment we overcome, we flow into in the path of the perception of our goals and the invention of our real functionality. So, permit us to forge in advance, undeterred through way of the usage of the worrying conditions that lie ahead, and encompass a future full of triumph and growth.

Embracing Discomfort: Building Resilience within the Face of Challenges

Life is a tapestry of demanding situations and uncertainties, and our capability to encompass pain is the crucial issue to building resilience. In this empowering adventure, we're capable of discover the transformative energy of stepping outside our comfort zones, handling adversity head-on, and building resilience inside the face of demanding conditions. Through actual-existence examples, we will witness humans who have embraced soreness and emerged more potent than ever. So, allow us to embark in this inspiring journey, expensive adventurers, and discover the path to resilience.

The Courage to Step Outside the Comfort Zone Real-lifestyles Example: Sir Edmund Hillary and the Conquest of Mount Everest

Sir Edmund Hillary, together with Tenzing Norgay, have become the primary climbers to advantage the summit of Mount Everest. In this chapter, we can delve into the super bodily and highbrow worrying conditions they confronted during their historical expedition. We will find out how they confronted their fears, driven their limits, and stepped outside their comfort zones to collect the apparently now not feasible. Hillary's tale teaches us that embracing ache and confronting worry is the gateway to first rate accomplishments.

The Strength to Persist in Adversity Real-existence Example: Nelson Mandela and the Fight Against Apartheid

Nelson Mandela, the long-lasting anti-apartheid leader and previous president of South Africa, endured first rate hardships at some stage in his conflict for equality and justice. In this financial ruin, we will witness Mandela's unwavering willpower and resilience within the face of prolonged-term imprisonment and adversity. We will explore how he used his time in prison to grow mentally and emotionally, transforming himself right proper into a photograph of preference and resilience. Mandela's tale reminds us that enduring hardships with resilience and backbone can result in profound personal increase and societal trade.

The Path to Growth and Learning Real-existence Example: Thomas Edison and the Invention of the Light Bulb

Thomas Edison, the prolific inventor, encountered endless disasters on his route to inventing the electrical mild bulb. In this bankruptcy, we will delve into Edison's incredible resilience and his ability to view failure as a stepping stone to achievement. We will explore how he embraced the pain of repeated setbacks, positioned out from his errors, and sooner or later completed groundbreaking innovation. Edison's story demonstrates that embracing failure as part of the mastering manner is essential for private and expert growth.

Thriving in the Face of Uncertainty Real-life Example: Apple Inc. And the Steve Jobs Era

Apple Inc., under the management of Steve Jobs, revolutionized the technology organisation with the aid of embracing disruptive enhancements and adapting to unexpectedly changing marketplace dynamics. In this monetary wreck, we're capable of find out how Apple navigated through difficult instances, embraced ache, and continuously reinvented itself. We will witness how their functionality to embody exchange, take calculated dangers, and innovate delivered approximately their notable success. Apple's tale highlights the significance of embracing pain and adapting to trade to thrive in modern-day day fast-paced international.

: Building Resilient Communities Real-existence Example: The Civil Rights Movement

The Civil Rights Movement in the United States fought in competition to racial discrimination and segregation, advocating for equality and justice for all. In this monetary smash, we're capable of witness the collective resilience of individuals who embraced pain to project systemic injustices. We will find out how their courage, unity, and resilience converted society and created a greater inclusive and equitable destiny. The Civil Rights Movement exemplifies the strength of embracing pain to force social change and construct resilient corporations.

Transforming Challenges into Opportunities Real-life Example: Oprah Winfrey and the Power of Vulnerability

Oprah Winfrey, the influential media rich individual, overcame a difficult childhood and severa private challenges to become one of the maximum a fulfillment and frightening figures of our time. In this financial disaster, we're able to delve into Oprah's journey of self-discovery, vulnerability, and embracing ache. We will witness how she used her very non-public memories and struggles to connect to others and inspire personal boom and empowerment. Oprah's tale teaches us that embracing soreness is the catalyst for transformative private boom.

As we quit this exhilarating exploration of embracing pain and building resilience, we are inspired by the real-existence examples of people who've faced demanding conditions with braveness and backbone. Their recollections remind us that actual boom and resilience are born from embracing ache, confronting worry, persisting in adversity, and adapting to alternate. Let us include pain as a catalyst for private and societal transformation, luxurious adventurers, and launch our entire capability. With resilience as our accomplice, we are capable of navigate any project that comes our way and emerge more potent, wiser, and additional empowered than ever earlier than. So, permit us to step outside our comfort zones, include ache, and embark on a adventure of increase, resilience, and boundless opportunities.

Chapter 6: Why Comfort Isn't Always Best

Life is entire of alternatives, and one in every of the most important alternatives we make is how we live our lives. For plenty folks, the correct lifestyles is one that is comfortable and predictable, with a regular ordinary and few surprises. After all, who does not experience the security and familiarity of a existence that we realize and love? However, as a extremely good deal as we may additionally want to live inner our consolation sector, there are times on the identical time as this method can hold us back and save you us from accomplishing our complete functionality.

In this e-book, we are able to find out why comfort isn't always the satisfactory preference, and the way embracing exchange can purpose a greater high-quality and worthwhile existence. We will take a look at the severa strategies that staying in our consolation area can restrict our growth, and why stepping outdoor of it can be the catalyst for personal and professional improvement.

Comfort Zones and Why We Seek Them

The consolation region is a intellectual us of a in which we experience secure, stable, and acquainted. We are looking for consolation zones because of the reality they provide a experience of manipulate, an area in which we sense we're able to are looking forward to the outcomes of our actions. This predictability may be a deliver of consolation, and it permits us to experience consistent and solid. However, whilst consolation zones may also provide a revel in of safety and predictability, moreover they can be limiting. When we stay interior our consolation zones, we also can skip over out on opportunities for increase and development. We may grow to be complacent, and our talents and facts can also stagnate. This can bring about feelings of boredom and frustration, that may ultimately have an impact on our intellectual and emotional properly-being.

The Risks of Staying Too Comfortable

Staying too snug also can result in neglected possibilities. When we stay interior our comfort zones, we may avoid taking dangers or attempting new topics, which can restrict our research and opportunities for increase. We may additionally moreover miss out on vital relationships and connections that could have a massive effect on our lives.

Furthermore, staying too comfortable can also purpose a lack of creativity and innovation. When we stay internal our comfort zones, we can also additionally depend on familiar strategies and strategies, that might save you us from growing new competencies and thoughts. This can be damaging to our personal and professional improvement, further to to our capability to evolve to converting activities.

The Benefits of Stepping Outside of Our Comfort Zones

While it may be horrifying to step outdoor of our comfort zones, there are numerous benefits to doing so. When we consist of change and assignment ourselves, we are able to increase new abilities, gain new evaluations, and amplify our perspectives. This can bring about non-public and professional boom, in addition to a greater experience of cause and fulfillment.

In addition, stepping outdoor of our consolation zones also can build resilience and self guarantee. When we are going via challenges and overcome them, we're able to increase a more experience of self-esteem and self confidence. This may additionally have a amazing effect on our highbrow and emotional nicely-being, further to on our relationships with others.

THE BENEFITS OF LEAVING YOUR COMFORT ZONE

In chapter 1, we cited why staying inside our consolation quarter can be limiting and why stepping outside of it could be the catalyst for private and professional growth. In this monetary wreck, we are able to find out the diverse benefits of leaving our comfort zones and embracing change.

Expanded Horizons

One of the maximum large blessings of leaving our consolation zones is the possibility to make bigger our horizons. When we attempt new things and expose ourselves to one-of-a-kind studies, we can gain a broader mindset on life. This can assist us increase empathy and know-how for folks that are extremely good from us, as well as a extra appreciation for the region spherical us.

Improved Problem-Solving Skills

Stepping out of doors of our comfort zones can also decorate our trouble-fixing competencies. When we come across new stressful situations and situations, we're forced to suppose creatively and find out modern solutions. This can assist us amplify a greater agile and adaptable technique to trouble-fixing, which may be priceless in each our private and professional lives.

Increased Resilience

Leaving our comfort zones also can build resilience. When we face new disturbing conditions and push ourselves out of our comfort zones, we boom a greater enjoy of self belief and self-efficacy. This can assist us get better from setbacks and conquer barriers extra effectively, which may be vital to carrying out our desires.

Personal Growth

Leaving our comfort zones can also be an important catalyst for private boom. When we venture ourselves and take dangers, we research more approximately ourselves and what we are capable of. This can help us increase more self-attention, shallowness, and self-self perception, which can be transformative in all areas of our lives.

Professional Growth

Finally, leaving our consolation zones moreover can be an crucial catalyst for expert boom. When we step outdoor of our consolation zones, we might also moreover come across new possibilities and demanding situations that can assist us boom new capabilities, benefit new reports, and improve in our careers. This can motive greater mission delight, higher income, and a greater pleasurable professional lifestyles.

OVERCOMING THE FEAR OF CHANGE

In monetary spoil 2, we explored the severa advantages of leaving our consolation zones and embracing change. However, many of us war with the concern of exchange, that could preserve us lower back from taking risks and pursuing new possibilities. In this monetary break, we will take a look at a number of the common fears that save you us from embracing exchange, and strategies for overcoming them.

Fear of Failure

One of the maximum not unusual fears that holds us decrease decrease back from embracing exchange is the worry of failure. We fear that if we strive some problem new, we will fail and be seen as incompetent or inadequate. However, it's far crucial to recall that failure is a natural a part of the reading device, and that we can regularly research greater from our disasters than from our successes. By reframing failure as an opportunity to take a look at and growth, we are in a role to triumph over our worry and encompass new annoying situations.

Fear of the Unknown

Another not unusual worry that prevents us from embracing exchange is the priority of the unknown. When we're faced with new situations, we can also moreover fear about what is going to show up, or revel in unsure about a way to navigate everyday territory. However, it is vital to do not forget that the unknown moreover can be exciting and complete of opportunity. By reframing our fear as satisfaction and focusing on the capacity advantages of taking risks, we will conquer our fear and embody new opportunities.

Fear of Discomfort

Leaving our comfort zones additionally can be uncomfortable, and lots of us worry the ache that includes change. We worry about feeling awkward, embarrassed, or out of place, and may keep away from new testimonies as a quit end result. However, it's far important to do not forget that soreness is regularly temporary, and that the benefits of stepping out of doors of our consolation zones can an extended manner outweigh the temporary ache we may additionally moreover experience. By reframing pain as a important a part of the boom approach, we are capable to triumph over our worry and embrace new traumatic situations.

Strategies for Overcoming Fear

There are numerous techniques that might assist us conquer our fear of alternate and embody new possibilities. One of the first-rate is to take small steps in the path of our dreams, in area of looking to make drastic modifications . By breaking our desires down into ability obligations and regularly developing our degree of chance, we are able to gather self belief and resilience over time. It moreover can be beneficial to are searching out assist from buddies, family, or a therapist, who can provide encouragement and assist us live responsible.

THE POWER OF SELF-REFLECTION

In order to go away our consolation zones and encompass change, it is important to make the effort to mirror on our desires, values, and motivations. Self-mirrored image can help us higher recognize ourselves and our goals, and can offer precious insights into what changes we need to make a very good way to benefit our dreams. In this financial ruin, we are able to find out the electricity of self-meditated image and the way it could help us encompass change and live extra exciting lives.

Understanding Our Values and Motivations

One of the most important elements of self-pondered photo is knowing our values and motivations. When we're easy on what is maximum crucial to us, we're capable of make greater knowledgeable selections and take moves which may be aligned with our desires and values. By taking the time to mirror on what motivates us and what we charge maximum in life, we will gain readability and route in our preference-making.

Identifying Limiting Beliefs

Self-contemplated photo also can assist us pick out out limiting beliefs that can be preserving us lower back from embracing trade. Limiting ideals are terrible or self-defeating thoughts that we preserve approximately ourselves, and may save you us from taking risks and pursuing our dreams. By reflecting on our mind and ideals, we're capable of select out the ones which might be protective us decrease again, and work to reframe them in a more excellent and empowering way.

Setting Goals and Taking Action

Self-reflection can also help us set huge desires and take motion in the route of assignment them. By reflecting on what we want to carry out and why, we're capable of set precise, measurable desires which are probably aligned with our values and motivations. We can also use self-contemplated photo to discover the limits that can be stopping us from engaging in our dreams, and increase techniques for overcoming them.

Strategies for Self-Reflection

There are severa techniques which can help us have interaction in self-mirrored image and gain greater self-attention. Journaling is one effective approach, as it lets in us to document our mind and emotions and choose out patterns over time. Meditation and mindfulness practices can also be useful, as they permit us to quiet our minds and recognition at the prevailing 2nd. Seeking comments from others can also provide precious insights into our strengths and areas for improvement.

Chapter 7: Developing A Growth Mindset

In order to encompass exchange and leave our consolation zones, it is important to growth a increase mind-set. A increase attitude is the perception that our talents and intelligence can be advanced thru difficult paintings and resolution, in preference to being consistent dispositions. In this financial ruin, we're able to discover the importance of a increase thoughts-set, and strategies for growing one.

The Importance of a Growth Mindset

Having a growth mind-set is critical for private and professional boom. When we don't forget that we're capable of beautify and increase our abilities, we're much more likely to take dangers, embody demanding situations, and persist within the face of setbacks. In evaluation, even as we have got a difficult and speedy attitude, we can be more likely to surrender while faced with barriers, or keep away from demanding situations altogether for worry of failure.

Strategies for Developing a Growth Mindset

There are numerous techniques which can assist us growth a growth mind-set. One powerful approach is to reframe our mindset around failure. Instead of seeing failure as a sign of our limitations, we are able to see it as an possibility for growth and analyzing. We can also consciousness on the manner of analyzing, in location of simply the outcome. When we cognizance at the strive we established and the development we make, in preference to genuinely the quit stop result, we're much more likely to growth a growth mind-set.

Another technique is to encompass challenges and take risks. When we step out of our consolation zones and try new subjects, we're more likely to develop new abilties and capabilities. We also can searching out out remarks and studies from others, as opposed to in truth counting on our non-public abilties. By seeking out feedback and analyzing from others, we are capable of advantage new views and insights, and broaden our competencies and abilties even similarly.

Finally, we are capable of exercise self-compassion and kindness closer to ourselves. When we're type to ourselves, we are much more likely to take dangers and encompass demanding situations, in choice to beating ourselves up for our mistakes or screw ups. By working towards self-compassion and kindness, we are capable of domesticate a extra superb and growth-orientated mind-set.

LEARNING TO EMBRACE UNCERTAINTY

Change may be horrifying, and one of the motives why is because it frequently includes uncertainty. When we step out of our consolation zones and attempt new matters, we don't commonly apprehend what the final outcomes is probably. In this chapter, we are able to discover the importance of studying to encompass uncertainty, and techniques for doing so.

The Importance of Embracing Uncertainty

Embracing uncertainty is vital for private boom and improvement. When we are inclined to take dangers and encompass the unknown, we are much more likely to discover new possibilities and tales. We can also increase new abilties and abilities, and benefit new perspectives on the arena round us In evaluation, while comfortable, we improvement.

We keep away from uncertainty and stick to what is acquainted and

May also additionally moreover miss out on the ones possibilities for growth and

Strategies for Embracing Uncertainty

There are severa strategies which can help us learn how to embody uncertainty. One approach is to exercise mindfulness. Mindfulness consists of being gift within the

2nd and accepting subjects as they may be, without judgment or resistance. When we exercise mindfulness, we are able to discover ways to tolerate uncertainty and soreness, rather than looking for to keep away from it or push it away.

Another technique is to reframe our mindset spherical uncertainty. Instead of seeing uncertainty as a horrible or threatening detail, we can see it as an possibility for growth and learning. We can remind ourselves that trying new topics and taking risks is a natural and essential part of private and expert growth.

We also can exercise self-compassion and kindness closer to ourselves while we are feeling uncertain. When we're type to ourselves, we are more likely to take risks and embrace the unknown, in preference to beating ourselves up for our errors or screw ups. By training self-compassion and kindness, we are able to domesticate a extra powerful and increase-orientated thoughts-set.

Finally, we will are looking for out guide from others. When we are going through periods of uncertainty or exchange, it is able to be beneficial to have a supportive network of friends, own family, or colleagues who can offer encouragement and steering. By seeking out manual from others, we are able to enjoy more confident and able to embracing uncertainty and taking dangers.

THE IMPORTANCE OF SETTING GOALS

Goals are essential for personal and expert growth, as they supply us path and motive. In this bankruptcy, we can find out the importance of setting goals, and strategies for placing and attaining them.

The Importance of Setting Goals

Setting dreams is important for several motives. First, dreams supply us path and purpose. When we've a clean experience of what we need to reap, we are more likely to live centered and inspired, and lots much less likely to be distracted or sidetracked. Second, desires help us to measure development and song our success. By putting unique, measurable desires, we're capable of see how an extended way we've got come and what sort of we've got got accomplished, which can be a effective motivator. Finally, putting desires can assist us to overcome obstacles and setbacks. When we encounter disturbing situations or setbacks, having a clean goal in mind can assist us to stay targeted and taken on, and to discover new strategies to overcome the limits that we face.

Strategies for Setting and Achieving Goals

There are several techniques which can help us to set and achieve our desires. One approach is to make our goals unique and measurable. Rather than placing vague or well-known dreams, which includes "be more a success," we are capable of set precise goals, in conjunction with "boom my profits with the aid of 20% this yr." This manner, we're able to measure our development and track our achievement.

Another approach is to break our desires down into smaller, greater potential steps. When we set massive or bold goals, it can be overwhelming or discouraging to recall all the artwork that we need to do to benefit them. By breaking our dreams down into smaller steps, we are able to make the technique extra achievable and much less daunting.

We also can exercise power of thoughts and self-motivation even as operating towards our dreams. Setting dreams is one element, but certainly following thru and engaging in them is every extraordinary. By education willpower and self-motivation, we're able to stay targeted and encouraged, despite the fact that the going receives tough.

Finally, we will are attempting to find out help from others whilst strolling in the direction of our goals. Having a supportive community of buddies, family, or colleagues can be beneficial for staying inspired and heading in the right direction. By sharing our dreams with others, we will advantage responsibility and encouragement, that could assist us to live dedicated and focused.

BUILDING A SUPPORT SYSTEM

Having a guide device is important for personal and professional fulfillment. In this financial ruin, we can discover the significance of constructing a help machine, and techniques for cultivating and maintaining strong relationships with others.

The Importance of Building a Support System

Having a manual machine is essential for severa motives. First, a guide tool can offer us with emotional and social resource. When we're going thru tough times, having humans in our lives who care about us and may offer us a listening ear or a kind phrase could make a large difference. Second, a assist machine can offer us with realistic help. Whether we want help with a venture or a undertaking, or recommendation on a way to control a difficult state of affairs, having human beings in our lives who can offer us guidance and help may be beneficial. Finally, a guide gadget can provide us with motivation and responsibility. When we have people in our lives who agree with in us and our dreams, we're more likely to live inspired and on route.

Strategies for Building and Maintaining a Support System

There are numerous strategies that may assist us to construct and keep a strong help device. One method is to be intentional approximately the relationships that we cultivate. Rather than just counting on risk or condition to carry human beings into our lives, we're capable of actively are searching out out and broaden relationships with those who percentage our values and interests.

Another method is to be a extraordinary listener and supporter to others. When we provide our non-public useful useful resource and encouragement to others, we're much more likely to get keep of it in move once more. By being a tremendous listener and showing empathy and kindness to others, we are able to assemble sturdy and lasting relationships.

We also can take advantage of era and social media to hook up with others. Social media structures like Facebook, Twitter, and LinkedIn may be incredible for constructing and maintaining expert connections, whilst texting and video calls can assist us to live in touch with pals and circle of relatives who stay a ways away.

Finally, we are capable of make the effort to stay in touch with the humans in our aid device. Whether we time table everyday check-ins or discover time for social events and outings, staying related with the people who rely to us can assist us to construct and maintain sturdy and lasting relationships.

THE BENEFITS OF TRYING NEW THINGS

Trying new things may be horrifying, but it could additionally be quite profitable. In this financial ruin, we're able to discover the benefits of trying new topics, and the manner stepping outside of our consolation zones can help us to grow and amplify as individuals.

The Benefits of Trying New Things

Trying new subjects can also have many benefits. First, attempting new subjects can assist us to boom new abilties and information. When we attempt a few component new, we are compelled to analyze and adapt, that might assist us to come to be greater properly-rounded human beings. Second, trying new topics can help us to conquer fears and gather self assurance. When we efficaciously attempt a few aspect new, we are capable of experience a experience of success and delight, which can boom our self-esteem and self-self guarantee.

Trying new matters can also increase our perspectives and help us to expand empathy and understanding for others. When we attempt some element new, we're regularly exposed to new people, cultures, and techniques of thinking, which could assist us to extend our worldview and make bigger a greater appreciation for range. Finally, attempting new matters can simply be amusing and exciting. Trying new reviews can assist us to interrupt out of our every day physical activities and enjoy life in new and thrilling strategies.

Strategies for Trying New Things

Trying new topics may be daunting, however there are techniques that may help us to overcome our fears and take the leap. One technique is to begin small. Rather than searching out to tackle a large, daunting task , we're capable of start by means of the use of way of trying a few aspect small and doable. This can help us to assemble self perception and momentum, and make it less complicated to cope with larger demanding situations in a while.

Another technique is to set desires and make a plan. By putting easy goals for ourselves and breaking them down into ability steps, we are capable of make trying new matters revel in a exquisite deal much less overwhelming and additional possible. We can also are seeking out for our guide and encouragement from others. By surrounding ourselves with those who bear in mind in us and our goals, we will experience greater confident and prompted to take dangers and attempt new matters.

Chapter 8: Navigating Setbacks And Challenges

The first step in navigating setbacks and challenges is too well known and take shipping of them. We cannot control every detail of our lives, and setbacks and demanding situations will usually upward thrust up. By acknowledging and accepting these limitations, we can start to technique them with a boom attitude and a willingness to take a look at and adapt.

The next step is to take a look at from setbacks and disturbing conditions. Rather than viewing them as failures or setbacks, we can view them as opportunities for growth and studying. We can ask ourselves, "What can I observe from this enjoy?" or "How can I use this experience to end up stronger or extra resilient?" It is likewise crucial to workout self-care within the direction of instances of setback and undertaking. This may also encompass taking time to rest and recharge, searching for guide from pals or family, or carrying out sports activities that carry us pleasure and achievement. By searching after ourselves, we are able to build resilience and better navigate destiny traumatic conditions.

Strategies for Navigating Setbacks and Challenges

One method for navigating setbacks and stressful situations is to attention on the subjects we are able to manage. When confronted with a setback or venture, it may be easy to feel overwhelmed or helpless. However, via using focusing at the matters we are able to manage, which incorporates our mind-set, attempt, and movements, we can regain a revel in of enterprise and empowerment.

Another method is to reframe setbacks and demanding conditions as possibilities for growth. Rather than viewing setbacks and stressful conditions as insurmountable limitations, we will reframe them as opportunities to have a observe and broaden. By reframing setbacks and demanding situations in this way, we can collect resilience and extend a growth attitude.

THE ROLE OF SELF-CARE IN CHANGE

As we embody trade and step outside of our comfort zones, it's far important to prioritize self-care. In this financial ruin, we are able to find out the position of self-care within the method of alternate, and the way looking after ourselves can assist us to navigate stressful situations and gain our desires.

The Role of Self-Care in Change

When we're going through intervals of change, it is simple to turn out to be overwhelmed or confused. Prioritizing self-care can help us to control those emotions and live grounded. By looking after ourselves, we are able to construct resilience and higher address the disturbing situations that include exchange.

Self-care also can assist us to stay centered and stimulated as we artwork in the direction of our dreams. When we are feeling bodily, mentally, and emotionally healthy, we are more likely so that you can placed in the effort required to gather our dreams. Self-care can help us to keep our electricity stages and avoid burnout, allowing us to stay targeted on our priorities.

In addition, self-care can help us to assemble self-attention and enhance our relationships with ourselves and others. When we take time to mirror on our goals and engage in sports that convey us satisfaction and success, we're better able to recognize ourselves and our values. This, in flip, can help us to construct more potent relationships with others and make alternatives that align with our values and priorities.

Strategies for Practicing Self-Care within the direction of Change

There are many strategies that we're able to use to prioritize self-care in the direction of intervals of exchange. These may encompass:

Setting apart time every day for self-care sports sports, which includes exercise or meditation

Seeking guide from pals or family people

Engaging in sports that convey us satisfaction and achievement, collectively with innovative pastimes or interests

Prioritizing rest and relaxation, which includes taking breaks at some point of the day or getting sufficient sleep at night time time

Engaging in sports activities that promote bodily health, alongside aspect ingesting a healthy diet plan and getting ordinary exercise

RECOGNIZING AND OVERCOMING LIMITING BELIEFS

When it involves making adjustments in our lives, our beliefs play a critical function. Our beliefs form our thoughts, behaviors, and actions, and may every help or avert our capability to transport beyond our comfort zones. In this chapter, we can explore the idea of restricting beliefs and strategies for recognizing and overcoming them.

The Impact of Limiting Beliefs on Change

Limiting beliefs can also moreover have a large effect on our capacity to include alternate and step out of doors of our consolation zones. When we accept as true with that we are not able to accomplishing our dreams, we also can experience hesitant to reap this or attempt new matters. Similarly, at the same time as we agree with that others are not supportive or that the world is a harsh and unforgiving area, we may additionally additionally revel in discouraged or hopeless.

Limiting beliefs can also seem as self-sabotage. When we keep in mind that we are not really worth of fulfillment or that we're high-quality to fail, we might also engage in behaviors that undermine our development. For instance, we might also furthermore procrastinate, keep away from taking dangers, or give up while faced with worrying conditions.

Recognizing and Overcoming Limiting Beliefs

The first step in overcoming restricting ideals is to emerge as aware of them. This requires self-contemplated photo and a willingness to project our personal beliefs. We can start thru the use of asking ourselves questions along aspect:

What beliefs do I hold approximately myself, others, or the world round me?

Where did the ones ideals come from?

How do those ideals effect my thoughts, behaviors, and actions?

Are those ideals serving me, or are they retaining me again?

Once we've got identified our restricting ideals, we will begin to mission them. This might also moreover encompass looking for proof that contradicts our beliefs, reframing our thoughts in a more nice way, or actively searching out studies that undertaking our ideals.

Another effective approach for overcoming restricting beliefs is to are looking for aid from others. This can also encompass operating with a therapist or train, turning into a member of a guide organization, or looking for mentors who've correctly conquer similar beliefs.

FINDING YOUR PASSION AND PURPOSE

Finding our passion and reason in existence can be a powerful motivator for leaving our consolation zones and embracing alternate. When we have were given a enjoy of cause and direction, we are more likely to take dangers and pursue our dreams with strength of will and enthusiasm. In this economic ruin, we are capable of discover strategies for discovering our passions and figuring out our life's cause.

Discovering Your Passion

Discovering our ardour requires self-exploration and a willingness to try new subjects. We can start with the useful resource of asking ourselves questions including:

What sports do I revel in doing?

What hobbies or pursuits have I continuously been attracted to?

What am I obviously right at?

What sports activities do I lose tune of time doing? Step outside of our comfort zones. This cans also moreover volunteering, or exploring new interests and hobbies.

Another powerful strategy for discovering our passion is to try new subjects and comprise taking education,

Identifying Your Purpose

Identifying our life's cause requires a deeper diploma of self-reflected photo and a hobby of our values, strengths, and goals. We can start thru asking ourselves questions which incorporates:

What values are maximum crucial to me?

What strengths do I very own?

What problems or problems in the worldwide do I revel in interested in deal with?

What legacy do I want to depart within the returned of?

Another effective technique for figuring out our purpose is to have a look at the intersection of our passions, abilities, and the wishes of the area. By finding strategies to use our precise capabilities and skills to make a super impact, we're able to create a sense of motive and because of this in our lives.

Chapter 9: Creating A Vision For Your Future

Creating a vision for our future is an essential step in the machine of leaving our consolation zones and embracing trade. When we've got have been given a easy idea of what we want to collect and wherein we want to transport in lifestyles, we're higher capable of make selections and take moves that align with our dreams. In this economic wreck, we are able to explore strategies for growing a imaginative and prescient for our future and turning our goals into fact.

Defining Your Vision

Defining our vision requires us to invite ourselves questions which includes:

What does success appear like for me?

What are my lengthy-time period dreams?

What do I want to advantage in my private and expert lifestyles?

What values are most vital to me, and the way can I stay in alignment with them?

Another effective method for defining our imaginative and prescient is to create a vision board or visible instance of our dreams and aspirations. This can help us to live endorse and targeted on our goals, even supposing confronted with challenges and setbacks.

Turning Your Vision into Reality

Turning our imaginative and prescient into truth calls for us to take intentional movement and make selections that align with our goals. This can also comprise stepping outside of our consolation zones, taking calculated risks, and searching out new possibilities. It additionally requires us to stay dedicated to our imaginative and prescient and persevere thru boundaries and setbacks.

One powerful approach for turning our vision into reality is to break our goals down into smaller, greater feasible steps. This can help us to live centered on our dreams and make improvement towards conducting them, even supposing faced with demanding situations or distractions.

THE ART OF LETTING GO

One of the maximum difficult components of leaving our comfort zones and embracing change is gaining knowledge of to permit bypass of the subjects that now not serve us. This may also moreover encompass antique behavior, relationships, beliefs, or possibly cloth possessions. In this financial ruin, we are capable of find out the art of letting pass and the benefits it is able to deliver to our lives.

Why Letting Go is Important

Letting waft is vital because it allows us to:

Move on from past hurts and traumas

Release horrible feelings which encompass anger, resentment, and worry

Make room for modern reports and opportunities

Find greater peace and contentment in our lives

Live in alignment with our values and aspirations

How to Let Go

Letting bypass is a technique that calls for time, endurance, and self-compassion. Here are some techniques for letting flow:

Identify what you want to permit flow into of: This may also encompass antique conduct, ideals, relationships, or cloth possessions.

Acknowledge your feelings: Letting pass may be an emotional device, and it's far important to well known and validate the emotions that get up.

Practice self-compassion: Letting bypass may be hard, and it's miles important to be type and compassionate to yourself at some degree in the system.

Find useful resource: Surround yourself with individuals who manual and encourage you as you let pass of the matters that not serve you.

Focus on the existing second: Letting skip calls for us to attention on the existing moment rather than residing at the beyond or disturbing approximately the destiny.

Create new conduct and sporting events: As you allow waft of antique conduct, it's crucial to update them with new ones that beneficial resource your growth and well-being.

BUILDING RESILIENCE AND GRIT

The Importance of Building Resilience and Grit

Resilience and grit are vital for absolutely everyone who desires to attain existence. When faced with setbacks and demanding situations, it is simple to get discouraged and give up. However, people who private resilience and grit are better organized to overcome the ones barriers and preserve shifting ahead. Resilience permits us to get better from adversity, at the identical time as grit gives us the willpower to keep going even though topics get hard. Together, those features help us to collect our dreams and lead a extra exciting lifestyles.

Strategies for Building Resilience and Grit

There are numerous strategies that may be used to construct resilience and grit. One of the nice is to boom a increase thoughts-set. This entails seeing demanding situations as possibilities for boom and reading in place of as threats. By adopting this mind-set, we're capable of technique setbacks with a feel of hobby and a willingness to examine. Another technique is to domesticate a enjoy of purpose. When we've got a clean feel of our values and goals, we are better capable of persevere inside the face of adversity.

Additionally, constructing a strong help device can assist us to construct resilience and grit. Having humans in our lives that take delivery of as authentic within us and assist us can deliver us the electricity we want to overcome barriers.

EMBRACING FAILURE AS A LEARNING OPPORTUNITY

The Importance of Embracing Failure as a Learning Opportunity

Failure can be a really valuable getting to know opportunity. When we enjoy setbacks or make mistakes, we've got were given the opportunity to study from them and make changes on the way to help us to achieve our goals inside the destiny. Failure also can assist us to construct resilience and grit, which are important competencies for everybody who wants to go away their consolation area and encompass exchange. However, that allows you to embody failure as a mastering possibility, we want to be inclined to allow cross of our worry of failure and undertake a increase mind-set.

Strategies for Embracing Failure as a Learning Opportunity

One of the most vital techniques for embracing failure as a mastering possibility is to undertake a growth thoughts-set. This consists of viewing failure as an opportunity for increase and reading, in place of as a sign of weak point or incompetence. We also can reframe our disasters via asking ourselves what we can study from the revel in and the way we can use those records to decorate inside the destiny. Additionally, it could be beneficial to be seeking out comments from others and to surround ourselves with those who will manual us and assist us to study from our failures.

THE POWER OF POSITIVE THINKING

The Importance of Positive Thinking

Positive wondering is vital for all people who desire to depart their comfort vicinity and consist of alternate. When we anticipate sincerely, we are more likely to take dangers and attempt new matters that can motive personal and expert growth. Positive wondering also can help us to construct resilience and deal with setbacks more efficaciously. In reality, research has shown that people who expect really are much more likely to attain their desires and experience more lifestyles pride.

Strategies for Cultivating Positive Thinking

There are many techniques that can help us to domesticate a more super attitude. One of the best strategies is to practice gratitude. By focusing on the subjects that we're grateful for, we're able to shift our interest some distance from terrible mind and emotions. We can also challenge our terrible mind with the aid of questioning their validity and replacing them with extra terrific and realistic mind. Another approach is to surround ourselves with tremendous human beings and to be looking for out effective reports that bring us pleasure and fulfillment.

CELEBRATING YOUR SUCCESSES

The Importance of Celebrating Successes

Success can be a prolonged and tough adventure, and it is crucial to renowned the milestones completed along the manner. Celebrating achievement enables to build self perception, boom motivation, and encourage others. Moreover, it offers a experience of achievement and fulfillment, making the journey worthwhile.

Recognizing Your Successes

In the pursuit of exchange, it is clean to get caught up within the demanding situations and neglect approximately the improvement made. Therefore, it's miles critical to reflect on the adventure and find out the successes completed. It can be useful to hold a magazine of accomplishments, regardless of how small, and revisit them at the same time as motivation and notion are desired.

Celebrating with Others

Celebrating fulfillment isn't always quite an awful lot personal reputation, but it is also an opportunity to thank folks who supported us along the way. Celebrating with others can assist to construct stronger relationships and encourage them to keep assisting us in our journey. It may be as easy as expressing gratitude or as complicated as throwing a celebration.

Maintaining Momentum

Celebrating successes provides a feel of feat and may be a powerful motivator to keep on the direction of personal development. However, it's miles crucial to maintain the momentum thru putting new dreams and continuing to paintings closer to them. Celebrating achievement ought to no longer be the prevent of the journey, but as an opportunity a stepping stone to similarly boom and improvement.

Chapter 10: The Value Of Rest And Rejuvenation

The Importance of Rest

Rest is important for our bodily, intellectual, and emotional fitness. Our our bodies want time to get over every day sports activities activities and recharge for the following day. Lack of rest can motive fatigue, reduced focus, and decreased productiveness, making it difficult to accomplish our goals.

Moreover, chronic stress may additionally have negative effects on our fitness, primary to situations which encompass immoderate blood pressure, coronary coronary heart illness, and despair. Therefore, taking regular breaks and giving ourselves time to relaxation isn't always only useful for our well-being however additionally essential for our functionality to hold making development.

The Benefits of Rejuvenation

Rejuvenation is going beyond honestly rest. It consists of taking intentional steps to attend to our bodily, intellectual, and emotional health. This can encompass practices collectively with exercise, meditation, spending time in nature, or carrying out progressive interests.

Rejuvenation enables us to revel in energized, inspired, and centered. It also can assist us to govern pressure, reduce anxiety, and improve our not unusual temper. By incorporating rejuvenation practices into our every day lives, we're able to help our journey of alternate and beautify our potential to face new worrying conditions.

How to Incorporate Rest and Rejuvenation into Your Life

Incorporating rest and rejuvenation practices into our lives may be difficult, specifically if we are used to continuously pushing ourselves. However, with intentional attempt and determination, we will make it a dependancy.

One way to begin is with the resource of putting apart time each day for rest and rejuvenation. This can encompass taking short breaks in some unspecified time within the destiny of the day to stretch, meditate, or take a stroll. It can also include scheduling time for exercise or undertaking a interest that brings us satisfaction.

Another way to consist of relaxation and rejuvenation is to prioritize self-care. This can embody practices inclusive of getting enough sleep, consuming a healthy healthy eating plan, and looking after our highbrow health via treatment or counseling.

The Benefits of Cultivating Gratitude and Appreciation

Gratitude and appreciation are effective emotions which have a powerful impact on our physical, emotional, and social properly-being. Studies have confirmed that folks who exercise gratitude and appreciation on a everyday basis have a lower risk of depression, stress, and tension, and have better relationships with others.

Gratitude and appreciation additionally help us to popularity on what we've got were given, in preference to what we lack. When we take time to widely known the good things in our lives, we experience happier and more content material cloth. This, in turn, leads to a more experience of purpose and which means in lifestyles.

Practical Tips for Cultivating Gratitude and Appreciation

Here are a few practical hints and sports activities activities that you could use to cultivate gratitude and appreciation on your each day lifestyles:

Keep a gratitude magazine: Take a couple of minutes every day to put in writing down down 3 belongings you are thankful for. This may be some thing from an super cup of espresso within the morning to a supportive pal or member of the family.

Practice mindfulness: Take time each day to be present in the 2nd and consciousness on the sensations spherical you. This may be as easy as taking some deep breaths and noticing the sensation of your toes at the floor.

Say thanks: Expressing gratitude verbally is a effective manner to domesticate top notch emotions. Take time every day to thank a person who has accomplished a few component kind or beneficial for you.

Practice self-compassion: Be kind to your self and exercise self-care. Treat your self with the equal kindness and compassion which you would probably offer to a friend.

OVERCOMING IMPOSTER SYNDROME

Causes of Imposter Syndrome

There are numerous motives of imposter syndrome, which encompass perfectionism, fear of failure, and excessive expectations from others. Individuals who have professional great fulfillment at an early age or who have obtained praise for his or her accomplishments can also be vulnerable to imposter syndrome.

Overcoming Imposter Syndrome

There are numerous strategies that individuals can use to conquer imposter syndrome, along with acknowledging their successes, reframing horrible self-speak, and seeking out guide from others. Additionally, focusing on non-public growth in vicinity of outdoor validation can assist people experience more confident and reduce feelings of imposter syndrome.

Detailed Strategies

Acknowledge your successes: It is important to understand your accomplishments and have a laugh them. This can assist to lessen feelings of self-doubt and remind you of your talents. Write down your achievements and evaluate self belief.

Reframe terrible self-communicate: them regularly to assist assemble your

Negative self-communicate can make a contribution to imposter syndrome. Challenge horrible mind via reframing them in a incredible moderate. For instance, in area of wondering "I do not deserve this advertising," try reframing it as "I worked hard for this marketing and I deserve it."

Seek help from others: Talking to others approximately your emotions of imposter syndrome will allow you to comprehend which you are not on my own. Seek beneficial aid from buddies, own family, or a therapist to help you art work thru your feelings and expand techniques to conquer imposter syndrome.

Focus on non-public growth: Rather than focusing on outdoor validation, together with praise or awards, interest on non-public increase and development. Set dreams for your self and paintings toward them. This permit you to revel in greater confident for your skills and decrease feelings of imposter syndrome.

The Importance of Consistency

Consistency is critical in relation to preserving exchange. We need to hold the present day conduct and behaviors that we have were given observed to lead them to a part of our each day habitual. It is crucial to endure in mind that trade is a slow system, and it takes time to shape new conduct. It is essential to be affected man or woman and continual and no longer give up at the same time as we're facing barriers or setbacks.

Setting Realistic Goals

Setting sensible dreams is essential for retaining change. We want to set particular, measurable, potential, relevant, and time-sure desires (SMART). When we set unrealistic desires, we're more likely to lose motivation and give up. It is important to break down large goals into smaller ones and have a good time our improvement along the manner.

Staying Accountable

Accountability is crucial on the subject of keeping alternate. We need to maintain ourselves answerable for our actions and are seeking out for resource from others at the same time as we need it. We can also find out an duty associate who can help us stay on the right track and provide us with comments and encouragement.

Maintaining Self-Care

Self-care is essential nearly about preserving trade. We want to take care of our physical, emotional, and highbrow health to have the strength and motivation to reap our desires. Self-care can encompass getting enough sleep, consuming a healthy eating regimen, exercising regularly, and taking breaks on the same time as wanted.

Continued Learning

Continued studying is vital for keeping alternate. We need to maintain learning and growing to keep away from becoming stagnant or complacent. We can have a look at books, take guides, attend workshops, or are searching out mentorship to preserve growing our skills and data.

Rewards of Embracing Change

One of the maximum essential rewards of embracing exchange is non-public boom. When we mission ourselves and step outside our consolation zones, we observe new abilties, gain new perspectives, and increase a more experience of self-interest. We grow to be extra resilient and adaptable, better able to manage some thing lifestyles throws our manner.

Change can also deliver us inside the path of our goals and desires. When we take risks and attempt new subjects, we open up new possibilities for ourselves. We also can find out capabilities and passions we didn't even apprehend we had, and locate new paths to achievement and achievement.

Another gain of embracing change is the effect it may have on our relationships. When we escape of our antique workout exercises and conduct, we create area for new connections and research. We may additionally meet new those who percentage our pastimes and values, or deepen our relationships with those we already understand.

Chapter 11: The Power Of Embracing Discomfort

Subsection 1.1: The Comfort Zone Paradox: Why Growth Requires Discomfort.

Beginner: Recognizing the Signs of Staying in Your Comfort Zone.

Picture this: You're nestled within the cushty corner of your consolation vicinity, in which the whole thing is acquainted, predictable, and secure. It's like sporting a snug blanket on a chilly day. But, proper here's the capture—even as comfort feels inviting, it could slowly remodel right proper right into a cage that inhibits your boom.

Are you playing it secure greater often than now not? Do you avoid conditions that make you slightly uneasy? If you nodded, you are no longer on my own. As novices, we will be predisposed to gravitate within the route of the familiar. We live with sporting sports, turn away from new critiques, and keep away from dangers. It's human nature, in any case. But have you ever ever questioned why tremendous mind, massive learning, and existence-changing moments often rise up outside this comfy bubble?

Think of the consolation region as a magnetic strain that lures you in with its warmth encompass. It's snug, sure, however it could stunt your development and limit your capacity. The properly news? You have the energy to break loose.

Intermediate: Understanding the Psychology Behind Comfort Zones.

Now, permit's dive into the psychology at the back of the comfort region. Your mind is a splendid creature, stressed out to protect you from harm. It prospers on ordinary and predictability to decrease strain. So, on the equal time as you challenge into the unknown, your mind's alarm bells begin ringing. "Danger, danger!" it shouts, freeing a flood of tension and uncertainty.

But right here's the twist: boom occurs even as your mind encounters a task. Those demanding jitters? They're truly a signal that your mind is gearing up for some thing transformative. When you step outside your comfort area, your brain office work new connections, adapts to trade, and expands its talents.

Imagine you are gaining knowledge of to revel in a motorcycle. At first, your mind protests, fearing a fall. But with practice, your mind rewires itself. Riding becomes 2d nature. It's the same precept while you embark on a modern day undertaking or meet new human beings. Your mind adjusts, learns, and grows.

Expert: Exploring Case Studies of Individuals Who Broke Free.

Let's take a captivating adventure into the lives of people who defied the gravitational pull of their comfort zones. Consider the tale of Sara Blakely, the founder of Spanx.

She had a ordinary task and no revel in in fashion or organization. Yet, she dared to dream and created an empire via stepping outside her consolation area.

Then there can be Elon Musk, who ventured past the realms of software program with SpaceX. He confronted setbacks, disasters, and naysayers. Yet, through pushing his limits, he revolutionized place tour and stimulated a generation to reap for the celebrities.

These people faced pain head-on, transforming traumatic situations into steppingstones. Their memories display that the route to greatness isn't paved with comfort—it's far strong through adversity, analyzing, and audacity.

Remember, ache is your compass guiding you in the direction of boom. Every time you feel those butterflies on your belly, understand it as a sign that you're getting ready to some thing extremely good.

Embrace the paradox: thru stepping outside your consolation place, you are now not dropping safety; you are gaining a international of possibilities.

As you keep your adventure through this ebook, you will find out techniques, strategies, and insights to overcome your consolation area and embark on a interesting day ride of self-discovery and private evolution. So, are you equipped to step into the unknown? It's time to project your limitations, smash loose from the mundane, and embody the pain that fuels your extremely good functionality.

Section 1.2: Embracing Fear as a Catalyst for Change.

Fear – it is that gripping sensation that knots your belly, quickens your heartbeat, and sends shivers down your spine. We've all experienced it. It's the strain that holds us again, whispering doubts and insecurities in our ears. But what if I encouraged you that fear, that very emotion that appears to paralyze us, may want to emerge as the spark that ignites transformation? In this monetary ruin, we are going to dive deep into the art work of embracing worry as a catalyst for alternate – a potential that is critical on the journey to stepping outside your consolation vicinity.

Beginner: Identifying Common Fears that Hold You Back.

Picture this: you're status at the edge of a cliff, looking down into the abyss beneath. Your coronary coronary heart races, your hands sweat, and a voice inner you screams to step again to safety. That voice is worry, and it is effective. As novices on this path, it's miles critical to apprehend the commonplace fears that frequently maintain us captive.

Imagine Sarah, a contemporary college graduate, eager to embark on her dream career. But on every occasion she considers applying for a interest, fear of rejection gnaws at her self belief. This fear is actual, and it's far ok. Identifying the ones fears is the first step to reclaiming manage over them.

Intermediate: Techniques to Reframe Fear into Motivation.

Now that we have diagnosed the ones fears, allow's reframe our mind-set. Fear, whilst harnessed correctly, can come to be a mighty supply of motivation. Think of worry as an strength deliver — just like lightning in a storm. It can both strike you down, or you can harness it to electricity your goals.

Take the instance of Alex, an aspiring public speaker. The idea of speaking in the front of a large target market used to terrify him. But he observed out that this fear wasn't approximately humiliation; it grow to be his frame's manner of making equipped him for a undertaking. He started viewing worry as a sign that he became pushing barriers, and on every occasion he confronted it, he grew more potent.

Expert: Strategies to Channel Fear into Productive Action.

Now, permit's assignment into professional territory. Here, we are no longer just reframing fear – we're wielding it as a device for green action. Fear will become your great friend, pushing you to new heights. How, you ask? It's all approximately channeling that energy.

Meet Maya, a pro entrepreneur approximately to release a groundbreaking product. The fear of failure loomed big, threatening to paralyze her improvement. But Maya hired a outstanding approach: she channeled that worry into meticulous planning. She visualized worst-case situations, and for every, she devised contingency plans. Suddenly, worry have turn out to be her compass, guiding her in the direction of whole education.

But that is not all — worry may be your thriller weapon close to preference-making. Jake, a inventory trader, located his coronary coronary coronary heart racing whenever he faced a unstable funding preference. He diagnosed that worry became his instinct's manner of putting forward ability pitfalls. By cautiously analyzing his reactions, he located to make calculated selections, guided with the resource of the very worry that used to hold him yet again.

Remember, embracing fear as a catalyst for change is a expertise honed through the years. It's not about eliminating fear — it really is neither sensible nor crucial. It's about gaining knowledge of the paintings of transforming that worry proper proper right into a using pressure, propelling you in the direction of your desires.

As you embark in this journey of harnessing worry, you can locate that ache starts offevolved offevolved to sense hundreds more exhilarating. Your heart pounding, your thoughts racing — those are no longer signs and symptoms and signs and signs of retreat, but indicators that you're on the point of some element exquisite. Fear will become your partner, reminding you that you're alive, which you're pushing barriers, and that increase lies simply past your consolation region. So, as you're taking your first steps within the route of embracing fear, take into account this: the electricity of trade is on your arms, fueled via manner of the very worry you idea held you captive.

1.Three The Science of Neuroplasticity and Unleashing Your Potential.

Beginner: Introduction to Brain Plasticity and Its Role in Personal Development.

The human mind is a surprise of adaptability. Imagine your mind as a sculptor continuously shaping and reshaping itself in reaction to your research. This phenomenon is called neuroplasticity, and it's far the critical issue to unlocking your untapped functionality. At its middle, neuroplasticity reveals that your thoughts isn't always a hard and fast entity however as a substitute a dynamic organ which could reorganize and rewire itself based totally mostly on the sports you interact in and the challenges you face.

Consider this: even as you first learned to enjoy a bike, your mind original new connections amongst neurons, developing a network committed to the complicated task of balancing and pedaling. As you continued via wobbles and falls, those connections grew stronger, solidifying your motorbike-driving talents. This critical principle applies to each thing of your existence, from studying new languages to adapting to unexpected situations.

Intermediate: Practices to Rewire Your Brain for New Experiences.

The adventure to harnessing neuroplasticity starts with intention and planned exercise. Much like a muscle, your brain responds to targeted attempt. To venture outdoor your comfort place, begin small. Engage in activities that challenge you simply enough to create a experience of pain with out overwhelming you. For instance, if public speakme terrifies you, hold in thoughts joining a small organization speak or taking factor in a workshop to grade by grade build yourself guarantee.

Diving deeper, mindfulness meditation is a extraordinary device for rewiring your thoughts. By taking note of the prevailing moment non-judgmentally, you improve the neural pathways related to cognizance and emotional regulation. Daily mindfulness exercise can't only decorate your capability to cope with pain however additionally pave the manner for profound private growth.

Expert: Harnessing Neuroplasticity for Advanced Personal Transformation.

For the ones well-versed within the artwork of stepping beyond their consolation region, neuroplasticity gives a playground of possibilities. Imagine looking to grasp a cutting-edge capacity, which include gambling a musical device or excelling in a activity. By dedicating targeted exercising, you could sculpt your brain's structure to optimize the precise areas required for your selected pursuit.

Take the example of famend violinists. Through relentless workout, they've got superior extra neural pathways of their auditory cortex, allowing them to understand and interpret music with superb intensity. Similarly, individuals who've conquered their fears and launched into audacious trips – like skydiving or conquering the degree – have revamped their brains to better method fear and anxiety, main to lasting emotional resilience.

In your very very very own lifestyles, keep in thoughts putting "neuroplasticity dreams." Identify areas in which you want to decorate your competencies or triumph over your fears, and create a plan for deliberate, steady workout. As you persist, your mind will adapt and rewire itself to assist your aspirations, propelling you to superb heights of private transformation.

www.ingramcontent.com/pod-product-compliance
Lightning Source LLC
Chambersburg PA
CBHW072157070526
44585CB00015B/1181